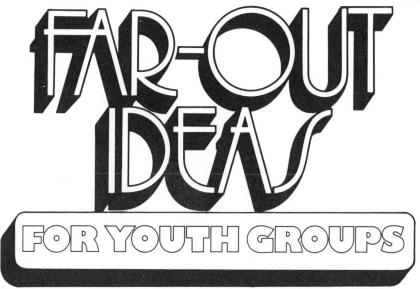

FAR-OUT IDEAS FOR YOUTH GROUPS

Compiled by

MIKE YACONELLI and WAYNE RICE

ZONDERVAN
PUBLISHING HOUSE   OF THE ZONDERVAN CORPORATION
GRAND RAPIDS, MICHIGAN 49506

Far-out Ideas for Youth Groups

CONTENTS

CHAPTER ONE

CROWD BREAKERS

CONFUSION

This is a great crowd breaker for parties or socials. Type up a copy of the list below for everyone in the group; however, no two lists should be in the same order unless the group is very large. The idea is to have everyone doing something different at the same time. Also, you are not able to tell who is winning until the game is over. The winner is the first one to complete all ten things on his list *in order*. Anyone who will not do what someone asks him to do is automatically disqualified.

1. Get ten different autographs. First, Middle, and Last names. (On the back of this sheet.)
2. Unlace someone's shoe, lace it and tie again. (Not your own.)
3. Get a hair over six inches long from someone's head. (Let them remove it.)
4. Get a girl to roll a somersault and sign her name here.
5. Have a boy do five pushups for you and sign his name here.
6. Play "Ring Around the Rosy" with someone and sing out loud.
7. Do twenty-five "jumping jacks" and have someone count them off for you. Have that person sign here when you have done them.
8. Say the "Pledge of Allegiance" to the flag as loudly as you can.
9. Leap-frog over someone five times.
10. You were given a piece of bubble gum at the beginning of the race. Chew it up and blow ten bubbles. Find someone who will watch you do it and sign here when you have finished.

SQUIRM RACE

Place a volleyball (or ball of similar size) between the foreheads of a boy and a girl couple. Without using their hands, they must work the ball down to their knees and back up again. Their hands must be kept behind their backs and the two must start over if they drop the ball. Couples do not have to be of the opposite sex. Two guys or two girls will work fine but a boy-girl couple usually adds to the fun of this event.

BASKETBALL AWARDS

The following "awards" may be awarded to members of the school or church basketball team at a "fifth quarter" social event, or youth meeting. The "trophies" may be mounted on wooden bases and the "plaques" on 6 x 12 inch pieces of plywood. All should be sanded, varnished, and made to look as much like the real thing as possible. Names may be done with a plastic label-making device.

1. *Player with the greatest offense:* Bottle of mouthwash on base.
2. *Player who smiles the most:* Tube of toothpaste on a plaque.
3. *Player who plays the dirtiest:* Bar of soap on base.
4. *Player with the most fouls:* A chicken (dead or alive) or free dinner at "Kentucky Fried Chicken."
5. *Most energetic player:* Vitamin pill on base.
6. *Best substitute player:* Book to read while sitting on the bench.
7. *Toughest Player:* Bottle of "Brut" aftershave lotion on base.
8. *Most injured player:* First-aid kit on base.
9. *Player with most baskets:* Easter basket full of candy eggs.
10. *Best dribbler:* Baby bib on a plaque.
11. *Best Jumper:* Frog (real or phony) on base.
12. *Best "clutch" player:* Old clutch or brake pedal on a base.

You may add more to this list with a little creativity. A "serious" trophy or award to outstanding players may also be added to end with a positive note.

CHARACTER ANALYSIS

This is good when members of a group don't know each other very well. Have each one write down some information about himself, on a sheet of paper, without his name. Suggested information could include:

1. Favorite food
2. Middle name
3. Hobby
4. Favorite T.V. Show
5. Age when first kissed
6. Most embarrassing moment

After these are filled out, the kids pass them in. The papers are shuffled, redistributed and each person reads the slip of paper he received to the rest of the group (one at a time). The group then tries to guess who the person is described by the information. This is a fun way to have kids get better acquainted.

STRAW MUMBLE

Have three guys come to the front of the room. Each gets a plastic drinking straw. The idea is to get the entire straw inside your mouth by chewing. No hands allowed. It is harder to do than you think. First person to do so, wins.

CHOCOLATE DONUT FEED

Tie a donut to several rubber bands so that the whole thing is about a yard long. Dip it into chocolate and while a person is lying on his back, have another person try to feed the donut to the first person. The donut usually bounces around like it's drunk, getting chocolate all over the person lying down.

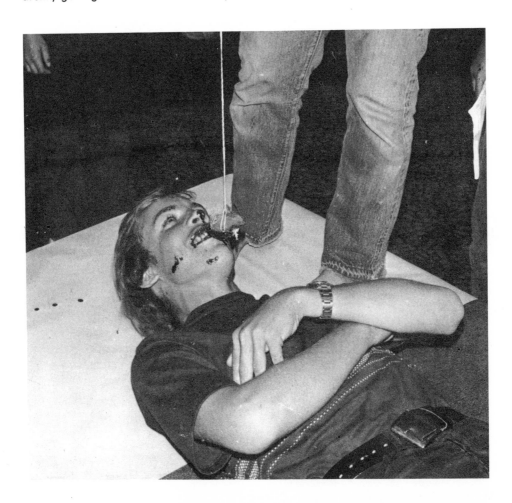

THE CONTAGIOUS GAME

Stand or seat kids in a circle so that all can see each other. The person on the end starts by describing his "ailment." For example, he might say, "My right eye twitches," and so everyone in the group starts twitching his right eye. The next person might say, "My left foot has the jumps," or, "I have whooping cough," etc., and everyone must start doing what he says. After a few people share their ailments, everyone should be jumping, twitching, coughing, sneezing, and having a great time. For double laughs, have someone film it on super 8 movie film to show later.

COTTON BALLS

Have a guy volunteer to see how fast he can pick up cotton balls with a spoon (blindfolded) and place them in a bowl. Blindfold him, give him a spoon, and have him stand behind a table with a bowl on it. Around the bowl, sprinkle a dozen or so cotton balls. (Let the volunteer see them.) After he is blindfolded, remove the cotton balls. Make sure he only uses one hand.

DROP THE BLANKIE

This is a great way to get everyone better acquainted. Before starting, make sure visitors are introduced, so that everyone has at least heard everyone else's name. Divide into two teams and have each team huddle at opposite ends of the room. Two people (neutral) hold a blanket in a vertical position, fully opened and touching the floor. Each team sends one person to stand one foot (twelve inches) from his side of the blanket. When they are ready, the blanket is dropped. The first person to say the other person's name correctly captures that person for his team. The game continues until only one remains on one of the teams. In case neither knows the other person's name, they are introduced and sent back to their teams.

I'VE GOT YOUR NUMBER

As kids arrive, each gets a number. He must wear this number in a conspicuous place on his clothes. Ahead of time, prepare instructions on little slips of paper. These are placed in a box. They should be things like:

> Borrow something from #1.
> Introduce #2 to #7.
> Have #6 get you a glass of water.
> Find out #12's middle name.
> Etc.

13

When everyone has his number, kids each take a slip of paper with an instruction on it. When they have completed the instruction, they come back and get a new one. At the end of the time limit (5 minutes), player who completes the most activities wins.

NOSE WASHING

Have three couples come to the front of the room. Place a glob of shaving cream on each guy's nose. From six feet away, the girls race to clean off the soap, using squirt guns.

STUMP THE BAND

If you have seen Johnny Carson play this game, you know how it is played. Your version of it might be to have the staff or sponsors of your Youth Group at the front of the room, while the leader goes to the audience to pick out volunteers, who try to name a song the staff doesn't know. The song has to be legitimate (no on-the-spot composing). If the staff can sing it, they get the praise and admiration of the audience (applause). If they don't know it, the volunteer must sing his song to win his prize. Possible prizes are:

1. A free chicken dinner. (Give them a live chicken)
2. A sleeping bag. (A "bed" with a paper bag "sleeping" in it)
3. Half a haircut.
4. A certificate for a free sewer inspection.
5. Candlelight dinner for two. (At the City Rescue Mission)
6. Answer sheets to 1903 math test.

Think of your own crazy prizes.

FLOURED LIFE SAVERS

Fill two pie tins or pans with flour. Drop several life savers in each and mix them in so they are not visible. Have two guys race to see who can retrieve the most lifesavers out of the flour in one minute.

DO I KNOW THAT PERSON

Divide the people into four groups. Have each group select one person and list 6-8 facts about him. Then have the recorder of the group read the facts to the other 3 groups. The object is to guess who the facts describe as soon as possible.

LICK SPLIT

A great way to divide a group up into equal and impartial groups is to give each person as he arrives at the event a jaw breaker. Later on in the program when you are ready to break up into smaller groups, ask everyone to stick out his tongue — different colors are displayed and different groups are chosen: By the color of their tongues!

WHY AND BECAUSE

Give everyone in the group a pencil and a 3 x 5 card. Have him write out a question beginning with the word "why." Collect them. Now have everyone write out answers on cards that begin with "because." Collect them. Redistribute them at random and have kids read the questions they receive along with the answer. The results will be hilarious.

FRACTURED FLICKERS

Contact the parents of the kids in your group and see how many short segments of home movie film you can get of the kids when they were very young. Assure the parents the film will be returned. Splice it all together and show it to the group at a party or social event. Have the kids try to guess each person when he appears on the film. Old home movies are great fun to watch, especially if you get some embarrassing shots of each kid in the group, as a baby or toddler. Some film will be super-8 and some will be regular-8, so you may need to make two reels. Only a short segment is needed for each person.

I'M DREAMING OF A WHITE CHRISTMAS

Choose two volunteers from the crowd. Give to one a Kazoo, and to the other a Slide-a-phone (available in most music stores). Have the crowd sing, "I'm Dreaming of a White Christmas" in their best Bing Crosby style, and then have an instrumental duet by your two volunteers. The results are hilarious.

JINGLE BELLS

This is a great way to put new life into an old song next Christmas. Divide into six groups and assign each group a phrase of the first verse of "Jingle Bells."

1. Dashing through the snow . . .
2. In a one horse open sleigh . . .
3. O'er the fields we go . . .
4. Laughing all the way . . .
5. Bells on bobsled ring . . .
6. Making spirits bright . . .

Each group is instructed to decide upon words, actions, or both to be done by their group when their phrase is sung. For example, the group that has "Laughing all the way" might hold their stomachs and say "HO, HO, HO." The entire group sings the chorus ("Jingle Bells, Jingle Bells, etc.") together and then the first verse. As each phrase in the verse is sung, the assigned group stands, does its thing, and sits down. Do it several times, getting a little faster each time through.

CHAPTER TWO

GAMES

BIRTHDAY TURNOVER

This game is similar to the old game, "Fruit Basket Upset." Have everyone sit in a circle with the same number of chairs as there are people. "It" stands in the center, without a chair. He calls out any *three* months of the year. After the last month is called, everyone who has a birthday during one of those three months gets up and tries to take another seat. "It" also tries to find a vacant seat. Whoever is left without a seat becomes "it." The big move is when "It" calls "Leap Year." *Everyone* has to get up and find another seat.

CINDERELLA

Arrange chairs in a circle. All the Cinderellas (girls) in the group select a chair. The Prince Charmings (guys) each pick a Cinderella and kneel down in front of her. He removes her shoes and holds them in his hand. The leader calls for the shoes and they are thrown to the middle of the circle. Then the Cinderellas blindfold their Prince Charmings. After each prince is blindfolded, the leader rearranges and mixes the shoes in the middle.

On a signal, all the Prince Charmings crawl to the circle and attempt to find their Cinderella's shoes. The Cinderellas can help only verbally, shouting out instructions to their men. After finding the shoes, the Princes crawl back to their girls (again guided only by verbal instructions). They place the shoes (right one on right foot, etc.) on the girls and then remove their blindfolds. The game continues until the last contestant succeeds.

CHAOS-VS-CONTROL

This is an outdoor spy game best played at a camp where there is plenty of room and good hiding places. It should be played at night and preferably in an area with a lot of trees, high grass, and the like. Divide into two teams: the "Chaos" agents and the "Control" agents. (You can name the teams anything. The names are not important to the game.) The Chaos agents try to leave the U.S. by reaching a landing strip where their planes are to pick them up. The Control agents try to capture or eliminate the Chaos agents by hitting them with a stocking full of flour. The set up should look like the illustration on the next page.

The Chaos agents are safe when in their own territory. They simply have to sneak through Control territory to get to the "airstrip" located behind Control territory. If they manage to get through, they report to a counselor sitting at a desk on the airstrip. When they arrive there, they turn over to the counselor a set of "secret plans" (an envelope marked "SST" or "APOLLO," etc.). The Chaos team gets 1000 points for each envelope delivered to the airstrip counselor. Chaos agents may then return to their own headquarters via a path around Control territory to get a new set of plans and try to sneak through again. Control agents may patrol that path to make sure Chaos people are only going back and not coming to the airstrip.

Control agents can only be in their own territory and they must try to spot and club a Chaos agent with their nylon (rolled newspaper, water balloon, paper bag full of mud, or whatever). If they hit a Chaos agent, the Control agent takes his prisoner to Control headquarters and the Chaos agent must give up his plans. The Control team gets 2000 points for each set of plans seized. The Chaos agent is then set free to try again. Adult Counselors should keep score, hand out the plans, etc.

You can use several large flashlights (controlled by counselors) to sweep the entire area to give a "searchlight" effect to the game. The two teams should wear different colored armbands to distinguish them.

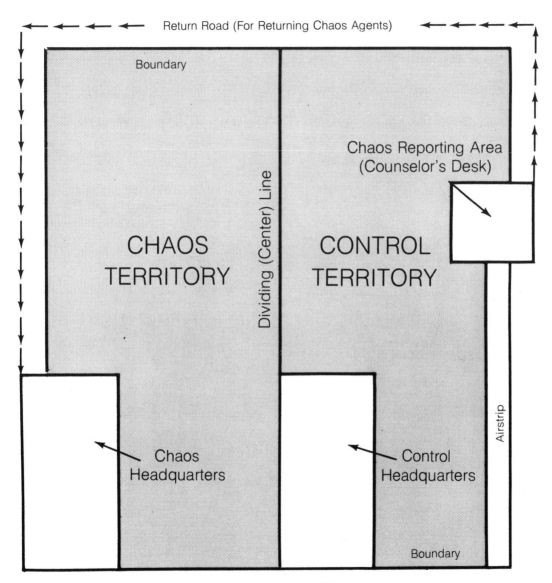

Return Road (For Returning Chaos Agents)

Boundary

Dividing (Center) Line

Chaos Reporting Area
(Counselor's Desk)

CHAOS
TERRITORY

CONTROL
TERRITORY

Airstrip

Chaos
Headquarters

Control
Headquarters

Boundary

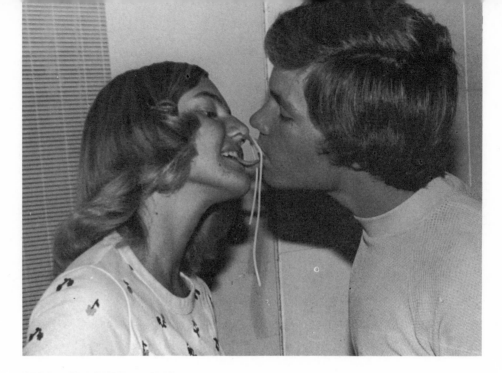

GREAT SPAGHETTI RELAY

Divide the group into teams. Each person gets a potato chip (the larger, the better). Each team lines up, and the first person in line holds his potato chip in his mouth. A wet spaghetti noodle is then draped over the chip and the person must run to a set point and back without dropping the noodle or breaking the potato chip. On returning, he passes the noodle on to the next person, who does the same thing. The game continues, and the first team to finish is the winner. The rules: (1) No hands are allowed. (2) If the noodle drops off, breaks, or becomes mutilated, the player must return to the line, get a new noodle, and start all over.

LAWN SKIING

For those who long for the mountain slopes or whose lakes and rivers may be dry, try this. Acquire several pair of water skis and remove the fins from the undersides. Get the necessary number of tow ropes or just plain rope (you'll need at least 40 feet), and begin your races. Local school or park lawns (just watered) provide a slick surface and kids pulling the ropes provide the power. Many variations are possible using slalom skis, skim boards, inner tubes, etc. and other surfaces besides grass are suitable. Events can range from slaloms to marathons.

TIN PAN BANG BANG

This game is similar to "Clumps." The leader stands on a chair in the middle of the room with a stainless steel pot in his hand and a metal spoon. The crowd begins milling around the room. Everyone has to keep moving. The leader then bangs on the pot with the spoon a certain number of times and then stops. The players count the number of beats and then get in a circle holding hands with the same number of persons as the number of beats. Those who are not in a circle with the right number of people when a whistle blows are eliminated from the game. This is continued with a varied number of beats each time, until all are eliminated except one.

WATER-BUCKET RACE

Use either a gallon paint can, a half gallon milk carton, or a gallon plastic milk carton. Put this object, empty, on a wire or thin rope that is tied at both ends to something solid. Do this over an open area (outdoors, of course!). Then choose up two teams. Give each one a water hose with water running through it. The object is to see who can push the container to the opponent's end first. The water from the hoses just happens to come falling down on everyone involved.

SUCKER RELAY

Teams line up. Each person has a paper straw. A piece of paper (about 4 inches square) is picked up by sucking on the straw and is carried around a goal and back. If you drop the paper, you must start over. Each person on the team must do it. First team to finish wins.

SOCK TAIL RELAY

Make several "sock tails," one for each team. A sock tail consists of a belt with a sock tied onto it, with an orange in the end of the sock, as a weight. The first person on each team puts on the tail with the sock hanging down behind (see illustration). Another orange is placed on the floor. On the signal, the player must push the orange on the floor to a goal and back, with the sock tail. If he touches it with his feet or hands, he must start over. First team to have all team members complete this task wins.

MESSAGE RELAY

This is a good team game. Teams divide in half and stand a distance away. Type out a crazy message on a piece of paper (one for each team) and give it to the first member who opens it, reads it, wads it up and throws it on the ground. He *runs* to the next person at the other side and whispers it in his ear. Then that person runs back and tells it to the next person and so on until the last person runs to the supervisor and whispers it to him. The team closest to the original message wins. Accuracy, not time, is most important, but they must run. Sample message, "Mrs. Sarah Sahara sells extraordinary information to very enterprising executives."

RATTLESNAKE

For this game of stealth and skill, you will need two blindfolds, a small plastic bottle (an Rx bottle works fine) with a rock in it, and a defined area for play. This can be done on large mats (of the wrestling variety) or on a carpeted floor. The referee blindfolds two people. One is designated the rattlesnake and the other the hunter. The hunter is spun in circles several times so he loses his sense of direction. We are now ready to begin play. It is essential that everyone remains absolutely quiet (everyone not playing is seated around the edges of the playing area). The referee says, "rattlesnake." The rattlesnake must shake his "rattler" and then try to escape capture by the hunter. The game continues with the referee periodically saying "rattlesnake" until the hunter captures the rattlesnake.

GIFT GRABBER

Here is a different way to "open gifts" at this year's Christmas Party. It can be used at any time of the year, actually, but it would seem most appropriate at Christmas. It works best with 15 to 20 people. Everyone gets a wrapped gift to begin with (they should be joke gifts and absolutely worthless, if possible, like an old shoe, an old motel key, etc.). After the gifts are distributed, deal out an entire deck of playing cards, so that everyone has an equal number of cards. The leader should have a second deck of cards that he keeps. When everyone has a gift and some cards, the leader shuffles his deck, draws one card and announces what it is. Whoever has that card (from the first deck) gives the leader his identical card and then gets to help himself to any other person's gift. Then, the next card is announced by the leader and the possessor of that identical card gets his turn to help himself to someone else's gift, and so on until no more cards remain. Players left holding gifts may keep them!

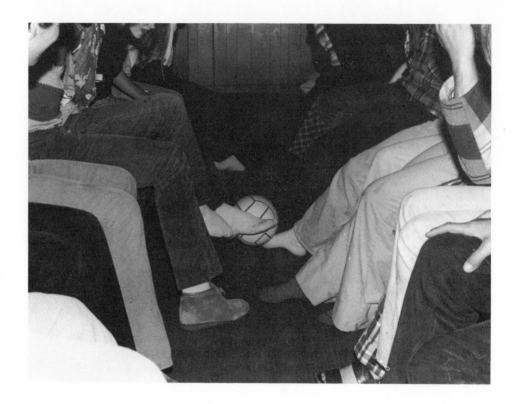

FEET-BALL

This is a good indoor game which is extremely active and requires real teamwork. Divide the group into two teams and seat them (in chairs) in two lines, facing each other. The object is for the teams to move the ball (a volleyball) toward and through their goal (at the end of the line) by using only their feet. Players must hold their arms behind the chairs to keep from touching the ball, which is a penalty. To begin the game, drop the ball between the two teams in the middle. The game may go on as long as desired. To avoid injuries to feet, shoes may be removed. Also, make sure the two teams are just far enough apart so that their feet barely touch when legs are extended on both sides.

KAMIKAZE

This is an outdoor game, good for camps or any group of 30 or more kids. Divide the group into two teams. One team will be identified by blue and the other by gold. These colors may be used with arm bands. Each team has a "president" who can only be assassinated by a water balloon. The president is seated in a chair which is inside a four foot circle, which is in the center of a larger circle, some 30 or 40 feet in diameter.

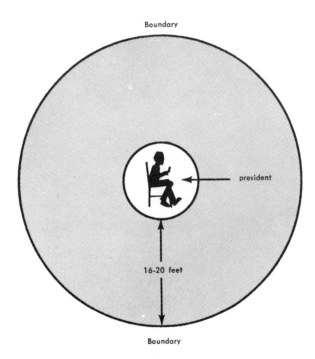

Boundary

president

16-20 feet

Boundary

Each team has the same set-up for his own president in two different locations. Both teams have offensive and defensive players. The offensive players each get two water balloons and may move in any part of the boundaries except for the area which composes the two circles with the president in the center. No person (offensive or defensive) may enter or pass through the two circles which surround the president.

25

The offensive players try to assassinate the president of the opposite team. They do this by tossing underhanded, a water bomb (balloon), from the edge of the outer circle. The toss must have an arch in it. If the balloon hits below the waist of the president, he is merely wounded and it takes three "wound" shots to assassinate him. A balloon hitting on target (above the waist) kills the president and the game is over (or if not over, points are scored and the team elects a new president . . .). An adult "judge" should be on hand to determine the legality of shots.

Defensive players are armed with a small paper bag of flour. Obviously, their job is to defend the president. They can "kill" the other team's offensive players by breaking the bag of flour on them, thus getting flour all over them. Offensive players cannot kill defensive players. They simply must run back into their own territory. Defensive players are not allowed into the other team's territory. (The playing area should be divided in half, with each team's president located in his own half of the total playing area.) When a defensive player kills an offensive player, he takes his armband and the dead offensive player must go to the graveyard and is out of the game. When all of the offensive players of a team are killed, they automatically lose the game.

The game is over either after a time limit or when the president is assassinated. However, to prevent the game from being over too soon, it might be best to simply call a time-out when the president is assassinated and the teams have five minutes or so to reorganize, elect a new president, get their dead players back in the game and then the game resumes. Also, during the break, scores are taken by the scorekeeper. Assassination of the president is worth 200 points and armbands of enemy players killed are worth 50 points each. New water balloons and flour sacks are passed out during each break (if any), which follows a president's assassination.

There should be at least four adult judges: One judge each for the team play areas and one judge to watch each president. Another person should be on hand to pass out flour sacks and balloons. (If a player uses up his supply at any time, he can go and get more.) This ammo area is "safe" and no fighting may be done there.

CRAZY CANOE

Two people get in a canoe facing each other. Each has a paddle. One paddles one direction and the other paddles the other way. The winner is the one who can paddle the canoe across his goal line about 20 feet away. It is very difficult and hilarious to watch. The canoe tends to just go around in circles. This can be done in a large swimming pool. In a large canoe, four or six people can play, with the two teams on each end of the canoe.

FAMILY GAME

This game is great for camps, retreats and special events and is best with a larger group (say 80 or more kids) in an indoor setting, such as a gymnasium or recreation hall.

Divide the group into "families" (8 families of 10, for example). Each family should represent a family immigrating to this country from another. In honor of their immigration to their new home, this game can begin with a banquet (sponsored by the Immigration Department), to which all the families are invited. Each family selects a mother and father and the rest of the children have to have some resemblance to the mother and father, i.e., all exceptionally fat, freckles, hats alike, or something. Each family must also prepare a native dance or native song from their country to perform at the banquet and also they must introduce their family by their full names to everyone else. The banquet may feature a variety of international dishes to make everyone feel at home.

At the conclusion of the banquet, the "Minister of Immigration" gives a little speech and presents each family with $2,000.00 in cash (play money made up of packets of $50, $100, $500 and $1,000 denominations) and gives "jobs" to about 6 members of each family. A "job" can be an old computer card with a particular occupation written down on it with the salary stated at the bottom. For example, a card might say "This certifies that you are a qualified PLUMBER. Salary: $8,000 per year." Each family is told by the Minister of Immigration that the Government would keep close watch on them and that only those families who really succeeded in their jobs would be allowed to remain in the country. After the banquet is cleared away, the game begins.

In the course of the game, 15 minutes represents a year. At the end of each year, the families meet together in a specified place to discuss what happened. At the beginning of each year (indicated by a whistle or bell) each member of the family with a job goes to an area of the room marked with his appropriate job description. For instance, there should be a medical center (for doctors), a trade center, a funeral home, etc. Also, at the beginning of each year, the father goes to the government desk and picks up his family's list of "problems" (see sample "problem card" below), which must be solved in that year. At this time he also gives the government a list of which members of his family have what jobs. In the first year, the problems are not many, but as the years go by, the problems get heavier and heavier. The list might contain from 5 to 12 problems per family the father has to solve. For example, his house might have plumbing problems — he might need to build a new bathroom. He might have a leaky roof, need new furniture or need the services of a doctor. There may be deaths in the family; grandmothers, uncles, aunts, children and a funeral director would have to be consulted, along with a minister, perhaps a doctor, hospital, lawyer, about the will, etc.

"Problem Cards" may look like this:

<table>
<tr><td>

Year One

Obtain a place to live

Get a job

Obtain for personal use
   form of transportation

</td><td>

Year Two

Pay rent if you do not own a house

Succeed at job

Wheels need balancing
   — see mechanic

Buy color TV — see Furniture store
                      Electrician

Girlfriend gets sick —
   See florist
      mother
      bank

</td></tr>
</table>

For every problem listed, there must be an appropriate "job" to solve the problem. Thus the father may either assign someone else or go himself to the various job areas and have the problem solved by a person qualified to do so. To get a problem solved you have to have a qualified plumber, for instance, sign that all the plumbing work has been done in your house and he may charge you according to how difficult the problem seems to be to him. The father then "pays" for the plumber to sign and the signature is put on the problem and at the end of each "year," the Government examines the problem list of each father to see that everything has been taken care of and only people who have a certain job have signed for the work done. If everything is in order, he is given the next year's list; if he does not have everything done, he may be fined several thousand dollars, maybe even up to $10 or $20 thousand dollars because of the seriousness of not getting certain things done. Then he may be given next year's list and he must go and solve the new problems.

There may also be a Government Employment Center where new jobs are for sale and occasionally it can be announced that there is severe unemployment and everyone has to turn in several jobs. This keeps the job market floating around, thus making it possible for families to improve their position — or to get wiped out, as the case may be. The Employment Center also sells B.A.'s, M.A.'s and Ph.D.'s for fairly high sums. If you are a plumber and have a B.A., you would get 25% more on your salary each year — the B.A. would be stamped by the Government on your job card.

If you got an M.A., you'd get 50% more on your salary and if it was a Ph.D., you would get 100% more.

If you have, say, 80 people, you would need almost 60 jobs, thus leaving some members of each family free to solve problems. Each "year" lasts approximately 15 minutes, with a 5-minute break in between before the next year begins, when the family may plan for the next year, look at the next year's list of problems and work out who is going to solve them. This is also time for counting money and for going to the bank where all salaries are paid. Thus, the bank has to have a great supply of play money. Occasionally, you may hit the families with taxes as well and they have to pay the Government a certain amount, a percentage of their income, or something for taxes. You can run the game for five 15-minute "years" and the family that comes out economically the best is the winner.

It is important to be fair when you are handing out the jobs at the beginning of the game, to make sure the higher-paying jobs such as doctors and lawyers and dentists are spread evenly among the families so that no family has a tremendous advantage to begin with. Normally there should be 3 or 4 doctor jobs, 3 or 4 dentists, etc., so that there will be a good deal of competition in bidding between members of a profession to solve problems. This keeps the prices down and provides a lot of entertainment. However, you may have several professions where there are only 1 or 2 jobs available, such as garbage collectors, funeral directors and ministers and this almost creates a monopoly for certain families, with prices sky-rocketing. You may want to do this, as it makes the game much more entertaining. This game can fit well into a later discussion on the family and enable you to talk about exclusive and inclusive families and the whole problem of competition in our society. "Do unto others as you would have them do unto you," becomes a very real principle when you realize that what you charge for your plumbing job, you may also get charged for when you are burying a loved one.

BATTLE FOR THE SAHARA

This is a game for two or more teams in an outdoor setting. Each team has a water container and must transport water across the "Sahara" (playing field), to fill the container. The first to do so wins.

Each team should consist of (1) a "general," (2) a "bomb," (3) three "colonels," (4) four "majors," (5) five or six "privates." For a smaller or greater number of players, more majors, colonels and privates are added with perhaps lieutenants as well.

Each player (except the general) has a water cup and each team has a water jug (container of a gallon or so).

There is a specified area where water may be obtained (which may be neutralized so players may not get caught while filling up). There is also a specified neutral area around the water jugs which are located at a fair distance away from the water supply. This distance could be 1000-2000 feet.

Each player (except the general) travels to the water supply area with his cup and gets it full of water. He then travels to the water jug and pours it in. While en route, he may be tagged by a player of one of the opposing teams. A tagging person must also have a cup full of water to make him eligible to tag. If a person tagged is of a lower rank, he must empty his cup. If two equal ranks are tagged, they part friends with their cups still full. If of a higher rank, the tagger must tip his out. Each person has an identity card with his rank marked on it. These may be written out in their team color.

All may tag except the bomb (although the private has no use for tagging, being the lowest rank). The bomb carries water but may tag no one. Anyone tagging the bomb is automatically demoted to private and has his cup emptied. Anyone demoted to private must give up his card to the bomb, who then turns it in to one of the referees at the earliest opportunity. (This keeps people in the game).

Any accidental emptying by an opponent gets the offended player a free escort with a full cup to his jug by the offending player. A general may tag without carrying a cup of water. He doesn't have one and is free to tag others at any time.

It is wise to set a time limit and the winning team is the one who either has the most water in their jug at the end of the time or who fills it up first. It is wise also to have referees along the route to make sure no foul play ensues and that offenses get free escorts properly.

CROSBEE

This game is a mixture of Frisbee and LaCrosse. All that is needed is a playing field, a Frisbee, and from 10 to 75 kids. Goals are set up at opposite ends of the field, two markers about 10 feet apart. Divide up into two teams. Each team selects goalies, and perhaps other positions such as defense, offense, forward, middle, back, etc. The two teams then line up on opposite ends of the field and the Frisbee is placed in the middle. On the starting whistle, players go for the Frisbee, and the first to get it may pass it to any other player on his team. When a player catches it, he may run with it, pass it, or down it, which is a "stop." (To down it, he simply falls on it.) Any player carrying the Frisbee may be "tagged" by a member of the other team and must then surrender the Frisbee to him immediately. (Referees should make judgments on this.) If a player downs the Frisbee before being tagged, he can then stand up and throw it to any other player on his team without interference. However, once the Frisbee is thrown, it may be intercepted. Also, a person downing the Frisbee may not score after downing it. Goals are scored by throwing the Frisbee between the goal markers.

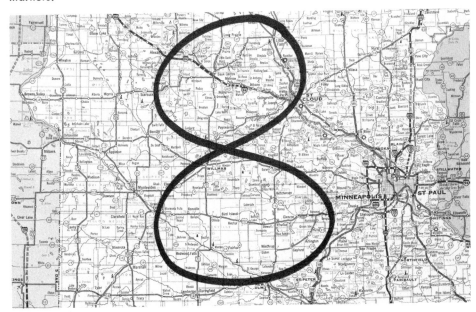

MAP GAME

This is a good indoor game for small groups. Obtain several road maps (all identical) of your state (or any state, for that matter) and before the game draw a large number, letter, or symbol with a pencil, such as a number "8." Make a list of all the towns that your pencil line crosses or comes near. Have the kids divide up into small groups and give each group a map and the list of towns. On "Go" they must locate the towns on the map and figure out what the number or letter is that the towns form when connected with a line. No guessing allowed (a wrong guess disqualifies them) and the first group to come up with the correct answer wins.

31

CLOTHESPIN RELAY

String a clothesline from one end of the room to the other, shoulder high to the average person. Place clothespins on the line. Teams line up facing the line. The object is to run to the line, remove one clothespin with your teeth (no hands) and bring it back to the team. All team members do the same in relay fashion.

WORLD WAR

This is a fun game for groups of over fifty kids. It is excellent for camps and may be followed the next day with a "total disarmament" game or "cease-fire" game which involves feeding the hungry, clothing the naked, or whatever. The purpose of this game is simply to win the war. This is done by destroying the enemy and capturing or killing their general.

NECESSARY PROPS:

(1) Water balloons. These are used as bombs, mortar shells, hand grenades, etc.

(2) Arm bands of various colors to identify everyone. For example, have a red army versus a blue army, by using appropriate colored bands on the right arm. Also another color of arm band may be used on the left arm to signify whether the person is air force, artillery, etc.

(3) Plenty of room to play (do battle) with good hiding places and such.

(4) Nonmilitary supervisors to make sure all the rules of the game are being followed. These people have the power to kill or heal at will. They should be equipped with whistles to start and stop the game, call violations, etc.

(5) An area marked off for the military graveyard.

PERSONNEL INVOLVED AND THEIR ROLES:

(1) "General." Each army has one. He wears either a red or blue arm band (depending on which army he is the general), plus a bright yellow band across his chest (Miss America style). He is the commander-in-chief. He may be killed by having his arm band or his general's band ripped off. He can't be killed by mortars, bombs, grenades, etc. (The idea here is that the generals are usually well protected in bunkers, not susceptible to artillery attack or strafing. They must be killed or captured only in hand-to-hand combat.)

(2) "Air Force." These are the only people in the game allowed to run. Everyone else walks. (The nonmilitary supervisors carefully enforce this. Violators are de-armbanded and sent to the military graveyard.) Air force people wear their band on their right arm and a sky blue band on their left arm. They may only carry two water balloons at a time. (Any air force person with more than two bombs is supposed to have crashed due to overloading and is de-armbanded and sent to the graveyard.) Air force may run in and out of any situation with two bombs. They may strafe any person except generals. (Anyone with water on them is considered "dead.") Air force may also run up to any person, take off either armband and run away. If the arm band which represents artillery, air force, etc., is taken, but the arm band signifying either red or blue army remains, that person becomes infantry. (Note: To capture a general, air force may run into general's bunker, tear off the air force insignia from his own arm, thus becoming a paratrooper. Once the air force insignia is off, however, the person may only walk and may carry no bombs.)

(3) "Artillery." These soldiers may only walk and are signified by a green arm band on the left arm and a red or blue band on the right arm. They are allowed as many water balloons as they can carry and may attack anyone with them. They can also function as refilling (rearming) stations for the air force. Once their artillery insignia is torn off, however, they may no longer touch the water balloons, even to hide or destroy them.

(4) "Infantry." These are the backbone of the armies. They only wear a red or blue band. They may only walk, but can kill anyone they meet. They should be used to protect the artillery and the generals.

FURTHER INSTRUCTIONS:

(1) Bombs and cannon shells (water balloons) are lethal to anyone who gets wet from them, including the thrower.

(2) Infantry may destroy the enemy supply of balloons by poking them with a stick. They may not, however, pick them up for any reason.

(3) Game ends when one general is either killed or captured.

(4) You can make the game interesting by setting sprinklers going here and there as mine fields. You can also rope off strategic paths as "radioactive" and anyone entering the area is dead and sent to the graveyard.

(5) Once dead, the person cannot kill anyone, and may not divulge any information.

FRISBEE GOLF

Lay out a short golf course around the area using telephone poles, light posts, fence posts, tree trunks, etc. for "holes." You can set up places as the tees or designate a certain distance from the previous "hole" (such as ten feet) for the starting place. Each person needs a Frisbee. The object of the game is to take as few throws as possible to hit all the "holes." Each person takes his first throw from the tee and then stands where it landed for his next throw until he hits the "hole." Of course, discretion must be used when the Frisbee lands in a bush or tree. One penalty "throw" is added to the score if the Frisbee can't be thrown from where it lands. The course may be as simple or as complicated as the skill of the participants warrants. Such things as doglegs, doorways, arches, and narrow fairways add to the fun of the course. Take three or four good Frisbee throwers through the course to set the par for each hole. It is a good test of skill, but anyone can do it. Two other games for a "Frisbee Night" could include a *distance throw* and an *accuracy throw* (like through a hula hoop from thirty feet).

PASS IT ON

The entire group forms a circle. Everyone is given an object which can be large, small or any shape (such as a bowling ball, a trash can, a shoe, etc.). On a signal, everyone passes his object to the person on the right, keeping the objects moving at all times. When a person drops any object, he must leave the game, but his object remains *in*. As the game progresses, more people leave the game, making it harder and harder to avoid dropping an object since there are more objects than people very soon. The winner is the last person(s) to "drop" out.

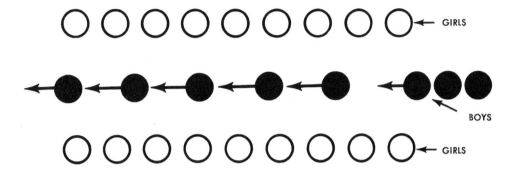

← GIRLS

BOYS

← GIRLS

RUN THE GAUNTLET

This old game is one of the best outdoor co-ed games available. Girls are given rolled-up newspapers, and they are lined up in two single file lines. The two lines are parallel, facing each other with approximately three to four feet between them. The boys tie balloons to their seats (on their pant belt loops) and must "run the gauntlet," that is, they must run between the two lines of girls who try to pop the balloons by hitting them with the newspapers. The object is to see which boy(s) can avoid having their balloon popped.

WINDBAG HOCKEY

A great way to play "hockey" in a small, confined area is to get teams down on all fours, and place a ping-pong ball in the center. The teams must then blow the ping pong ball through their goals (a doorway or the legs of a chair, etc.), without touching the ball. If the ball touches a player, he goes to the "penalty box" and no "goalies" are used. Two balls at once can make the game even more exciting.

BY THE "SEAT OF YOUR PANTS" VOLLEYBALL

This can be an excellent indoor game for large groups, especially during rainy weather. Divide the group into two teams. Set up a volleyball net in the room so the top of net is approximately 5 feet above the floor. Each player is instructed to sit down on his team's side of the net so that his legs are crossed in front of him. From this position a regular game of volleyball is played with the following changes:

1. Use a "light" beach ball type ball (or a "nerf" ball).

2. Use hands and head only (no feet).

3. All serves must be made from center of group, and overhand. Rotation would look something like this.

4. Because of limited mobility of each player a larger number of participants is suggested (20-25 per team).

5. All other rules of volleyball prevail.

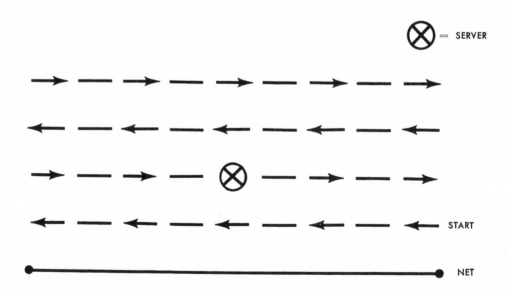

= SERVER

START

NET

DIAMOND SMUGGLING

This indoor camp game was developed for several reasons: (a) Often weather can ruin an outdoor game so that people get wet, muddy or cold. (b) Most camps have plenty of outdoor activities, so less tiring indoor games may be more appropriate. (c) Indoor games do not emphasize athletic ability — rather intelligence and sneakiness. Thus quieter kids generally like them better. They are very good, also, for adults. (d) You can control your campers at night far better with an indoor wide game than an outdoor one. There is virtually no safety hazard and you know where everyone is.

"Diamond Smuggling" is a basic indoor camp game. You will need a fairly large building for this game — a large lounge or dining hall with at least two rooms going off the main room. A school gym will also work.

The Dining Hall is set up as a coffee shop in Paris — one of the rooms off this hall will be the Police Station and another room (preferably not using the same hallway) would be South Africa (The Smugglers Den).

The campers are divided into two teams, the Diamond Smugglers and the Police. The Smugglers break themselves down into two groups, the diamond runners and the diamond smugglers, when they meet privately before the game in the smugglers den.

The object is for the whole smuggling team to circulate from their room (named South Africa) into the Coffee Shop (Paris) and back. The runners, whose names are on paper and are about 1/3 of the team, are allowed by the leader (an adult) to take a diamond (marble) out of South Africa into Paris where they must pass it to a smuggler, who then brings it back to the den and gives it to another adult. The team collects 5,000 points per diamond brought back to the den by a smuggler — not a runner — runners cannot bring a diamond back from Paris. That's why their names need to be written down so the adults in charge know the difference between runners and smugglers. The police never know the difference because they are never told, otherwise they could seize all runners coming in the door at Paris. All the smugglers and runners need to keep circulating back and forth from South Africa to Paris so the police never know who are runners and who are smugglers.

Paris (the main room) is set up like a coffee shop with lights low — some kind of music and food and drinks being served. Some kids may play games, etc. (A typical restaurant — coffee shop.) The Paris Police are everywhere in the room (and only in this room). They can arrest anyone they wish on suspicion of possession of stolen diamonds. To arrest someone a policeman simply places his hand on the shoulder of the person he wishes to arrest and says, "You're under arrest." The person must go with the officer to the police station — in no way can he resist arrest or try to ditch a diamond after being arrested. The police officer must accompany his prisoner to the Cop Shop. He presents the person at the door and a counselor takes the arrested man inside. The policeman is then free to go. The Cop Shop should be a secret place into which the Police can't see. Here counselors confront the arrested person and he must say whether or not he has a diamond. If he does he must give it up and the police get 10,000 points for seizure of the diamond and it's kept there. If the man does not have a diamond the police lose 4,000 for falsely arresting the man. In either case the arrested man is free to go out (preferably by another door) back into circulation in Paris.

This means that if a person is guilty he wants to look innocent; if innocent, he wants to look guilty.

The runners can pass diamonds any way they can devise — in glasses, under the table, in shoes, etc. They can drop a diamond off and let a smuggler know where it is. If a policeman can convince a runner he's a smuggler and get him to give him a diamond, he will simply turn the diamond in at the Cop Shop and the police get 10,000 points. If a policeman finds a diamond he does the same thing.

It is best to run the game 30-40 minutes and then have a half-time in which the teams change roles because the police have a tougher job than the smugglers. Then run the game for another 30-40 minutes. Use about 40 diamonds for a game, involving about 40 people on each team.

EXPANDABLE HOPSCOTCH

This is a grown-up version of the old child's game of hopscotch. Secure small size carpet remnants from any carpet store (they usually charge 10-25c for each one). These are the hopscotch squares. The game is played as usual, except that the squares are spaced further and further apart as the game progresses until the kids are jumping several feet between squares. It's good competition and is great for laughs.

WORLD-WIDE GAMES

A great source of table games, recreation-room games and the like, are available from the World-Wide Games, Box 450, Delaware, Ohio 43015. Write for a free catalog.

CHAPTER THREE

SKITS

THE GOBBLEWART

The skit begins in a pet shop where the proprietor is standing behind a counter. A woman enters the shop and inquires about pets, especially a dog about three years old and housebroken. The proprietor answers he is all out of dogs, but she may be interested in a "gobblewart." She wonders what in the world that is, and he points to a "blob" on the floor (a person hunched over on the floor). She exclaims that it certainly is ugly, but what does it do? He states that it can be very handy around the house for it will eat anything. Right after this, a girl comes running into the room screaming, "The gorilla is loose." The gorilla comes lumbering into the room (played by another person), but the proprietor calmly states, "Gobblewart, the gorilla." With this the gobblewart pounces upon and kills the gorilla. Just then the girl comes running into the room again shouting, "The lion's loose, the lion's loose." The lion comes into the room and the proprietor calmly states, "Gobblewart, the lion." The gobblewart pounces on and kills the lion. The woman is amazed and declares she'll take it. The next scene takes place at the woman's home. Her husband comes home from work and asks if she got a pet. She tells him of the gobblewart and points to the "blob" on the floor. He laughs and laughs and then exclaims, "Gobblewart, my foot." With this the gobblewart attacks his foot as he runs off stage.

FRONTIER PSYCHIATRIST

Annc.: Frontier Psychiatrist. This program is respectively dedicated to those brave pioneers, the frontier psychiatrists, who brought mental health to the West.

THE SCENE: The office of Dr. Tex Rorshalk: Frontier Psychiatrist.

Dr.: And so, madam, I want you to go back to the reservation and tell your husband he can walk if he wants to. It's all in his mind, purely psychosomatic. Your husband can walk if he wants to. Well, good-by, Mrs. Sittingbull.

Ah, interesting case. She can use a little treatment too. She's got a forty pound papoose on her back.

Oh, Nurse! !

Nurse: Yes, Doctor Rorshalk?

Dr.: Any more appointments today?

Nurse:	Let's see, Ben Cartwright at 3:00, McCloud at 4:00, and Matt Dillon is coming in at 5:00.
Dr.:	Ah, ha ha. Matt Dillon . . . very interesting case. Acute paranoia . . . persecution complex. Thinks Howard Cosell is out to get him. Eh . . . Now Nurse, I want you to . . . (gunshots).
Dr.:	What the . . .
Sher:	Doctor, Doctor.
Dr.:	Oh, hello, Sheriff . . . you're just in time for your appointment. Come in and lie down on the couch and . . .
Sher:	No time, Doc, we're in for a pack of trouble. The Ringo Kid just pulled into town.
Dr.:	The Ringo Kid?
Sher:	Yeah. The dirtiest, rottenest killer north of the Rio Grande. Why, he's a murdering outlaw . . .
Dr.:	Please, Sheriff — how many times do I have to tell you, there are no such things as outlaws. Just problem cowboys! !
Sher:	I tell you he's a killer! He came into town this morning and shot my deputy.
Dr.:	Now just a minute, I just saw your deputy, I talked to him.
Sher:	Did he answer you?
Dr.:	Come to think of it, no . . . thought it was some kind of mental block.
Sher:	Well, I'm telling you, Doc . . .
	(Shots and yelling offstage)
Sher:	Galloping coyotes! It's Buck! He's been shot! !
Buck:	He got me! The Ringo Kid got me! (Cough, cough)
Dr.:	Oh, you've got to do something about that cough. You know it's just nerves. Nerves you know. Just nerves. Nerves.
Sher:	Where is he now, Buck?
Buck:	He's in the saloon. (Cough, cough)
Dr.:	Maybe it's heartburn. Are you a compulsive eater? Now just lie down here and start at the beginning and tell me whatever comes into your mind. Now, what do you think about girls . . .
Sher:	No, no, no, Doc, he's been shot, Doc, and the Ringo Kid did it.
Dr.:	Oh! Well, I'll go into the saloon after him. Excuse me . . .
Sher:	Wait a minute, Doc, that's dangerous.
Dr.:	Sheriff! I am a Frontier Psychiatrist and that boy needs therapy. Nurse? Where's my notebook and pencil?
Nurse:	In your holster.
Dr.:	Oh yeah.

Sher:	But Doctor, you can't go in there. I tell you, he's vicious.
Dr.:	He's *not* vicious.
Sher:	Well, what would make a man shoot people in the back?
Dr.:	Poor toilet training — who knows — now if you'll excuse me please . . .
Nurse:	Be careful, Doctor, please be careful, Doctor, you know how I feel about you.
Dr.:	I told you before, Nurse, I'm just your father image. Now go finish the slip covers for the couch please.

SCENE II SALOON

(Piano playing)

SHOTS — Ringo enters — people screaming

Ringo:	All right — now listen to me. I'm the Ringo Kid. I'm the shootingest, fightingest hombre in the West. Anybody want to take me on?
Men:	NO, NO, NO! ! ! *(Group)*
Ringo:	All right, I'll tell you what, line up, you guys. Now when I count three you go for your guns.

(Bang, Bang, Bang — guys drop —)

Ringo:	One, two, three — Ya gotta be quicker than that. Ha, ha, ha, ha, ha, ha, ha. Hey, did ya see that, stranger?
Stran:	Yeah!
Ringo:	Bang! I don't like witnesses. All right, piano player, let's have a tune. *(Piano plays, then stops suddenly)*
Dr.:	Howdy, Ringo Kid.
Ringo:	Huh? Who are you?
Dr.:	*(Walks up)* Doctor Tex Rorshalk, Frontier Psychiatrist. Have couch, will travel.
Ringo:	What?
Dr.:	Now, what seems to be your problem?
Ringo:	Problem? I gotta itchy trigger finger.
Dr.:	Oh! That's not my field. Try a dermatologist.
Ringo:	*Wait a minute* — just what do you want?
Dr.:	I want to help you! ! !
Ringo:	Aha! I got you figured. Just a cheap analyst trying to make a reputation. Awright, start dancing! ! ! Head shrinker! ! ! *(Points gun and shoots)*
Dr.:	Poor Ringo Kid. You're just an angry little boy lashing out at the world with your six gun. Hmm Hmmm
Ringo:	I'm gonna kill you.
Dr:	Oh no! ! A textbook case. Ha Ha! Wait till I write the boys in Vienna. They'll flip.

Ringo: Awright, you asked for it. *(Points gun — shoots)*
Dr.: You're insecure, aren't you?
Ringo: What?
Dr.: You're full of frustration, and aggressive hostilities and it's all an artificial barrier to mask your inhibitions and your massive inferiority complex.
Ringo: You trying to tell me I'm crazy?
Dr.: Oh please, Ringo — we don't use words like *crazy* any more. Let me simply say that you're suffering from a traumatic dislocation of your emotional processes.
Ringo: Well, what does that mean?
Dr.: You're a nut!! You're crazy in the coconut!!
Ringo: Awright.
Dr.: You're machuga!!
Ringo: Awright, awright, you can talk to my gun.
Dr.: Ha, ha, ha — That's not a gun.
Ringo: It isn't?
Dr.: Of course not. It's a symbol.
Ringo: A symbol?
Dr.: A symbol of your inability to cope with reality. Now give me that symbol.
Ringo: Uh, here you are.
Dr.: Now the other symbol?
Ringo: Here.
Dr.: Hmph. You're a good man, Ringo, and I can bring out that goodness.
Ringo: Ya ya ya can?
Dr.: All you have to do is talk it out. Now lie down on the bar.
Ringo: Uh, all right, Doctor. *(Music cuts in — organ —)*
Dr.: Now, tell me Ringo, when did you first discover you hated your horse?
Ringo: But I don't hate my horse.
Dr.: Ah! Well, does your horse hate you?
Ringo: Well, why should my horse hate me?
Dr.: Well, you sit on him, you make him live in a stable, you feed him oats. Don't you think it logical that the beast should harbor some resentment?
Ringo: Well, I — I guess so.
Dr.: Did anything unusual happen to you as a child?
Ringo: Well, let me think. Oh yeah! Yeah! When I was eight years old, my home ran away from me.
Dr.: You mean, you ran away from home?

Ringo:	No, my home ran away from me. We lived in a covered wagon and I fell out.
Dr.:	Ah ha!! Ringola, Tingola — I think I have solved your problem. Your hostility to everyone is a minification of rejection. You have hallucinations that people don't like you and that is why you shoot them. If you act friendly to them, they will act friendly to you.
Ringo:	You mean, if I like them they're gonna like me?
Dr.:	Siggy Freud couldn't have put it better.
Ringo:	Doctor! How can I ever thank you?
Dr.:	You can pay me. I don't want to feel rejected.
Ringo:	Oh! From now on I'm gonna love everybody.
Dr.:	That's it!
Ringo:	Hello, bartender, glad to see ya!!
Bar:	Howdy!!!!
Ringo:	Hey there, friend, pleased to meetcha!!!
Friend:	Oh! How're you?
Ringo:	Oh! Here comes the Sheriff. Hello there, Sheriff — glad to see you. (Sheriff shoots Ringo)
Dr.:	Sheriff, why did you shoot that well-adjusted cowpoke?
Sher:	I don't know, I just shot him. Something came over me, Doc!!!
Dr.:	I see. Uh, give me that symbol.
Sher:	Here you are.
Dr.:	Now lie down on the bar.
Sher:	Ahhh.
Dr.:	Now tell me, when did you first discover you hated your horse? (Music)
Sher:	I don't hate my horse.
Dr.:	Then, does your horse hate you?

TUG-O-WAR SKIT

You'll need a room with two doors up front or a room divider, which will block out the view of the audience. This skit should take place while someone else is talking, so that it distracts the attention of the audience. A boy will come out of one of the doors tugging for all he's worth on a heavy rope. He struggles with this while pulling it across the stage and out the other door. A second or two later, as soon as he's disappeared from sight, and while the rope is still moving across the stage, he reappears in the first door on the other end of the same rope, except this time he's pulling vainly against the tugging as he is dragged across the stage and out the second door.

HUNG-UP ANNOUNCEMENTS

For a "change of pace" at announcement time, try this little skit. Have a piece of rope strung across the front of the room and at the appropriate time, have a guy (dressed up like an old lady) walk in with a clothesbasket. He (She) proceeds to hang up her laundry on the clothesline, with announcements written on each article of clothing. The idea is to take the audience by total surprise. The guy should really "ham it up" and act like a sloppy old lady, dropping the clothes, blowing her nose on them, etc.

"AND THE LAMP WENT OUT"

CAST OF CHARACTERS

1. The Reader ....Narration
2. Evelyn DeVere ....The Heroine
3. Ralph Grayson ....The Hero
4. Mrs. DeVere ....Evelyn's Mother
5. Herbert Vanderslice ....The Villain

SETTING

The library of the DeVere Home.

PROPS

1. False arm to fit under Mother's sweater or dress sleeve.
2. A small pail.
3. A small sponge filled with water concealed in handkerchief.
4. A whisk broom.
5. A traveling bag or briefcase.
6. Large clock.
7. Calendar.
8. Thermometer.
9. Photograph.
10. Needlework for Mother.
11. Lamp to "go out."

PROPS OFF STAGE

1. Broom.
2. Pans or drums for thunder.
3. Branches of tree to wave.
4. Moon made of tin or cardboard covered with foil.
5. Comic book for Evelyn.
6. Strong flashlight.
7. Red paper heart for Ralph.
8. Chains.
9. Sign with "time" written on it.

INSTRUCTIONS

The following script is to be read by the Reader. At each numbered place in the script, the characters or stagehands perform the "actions" as listed after the script. "Ham" acting is essential to make the skit as ridiculous as possible.

SCRIPT

(The story read by the Reader)

Fiercely the storm raged — the rain fell in torrents, the trees were lashed by the fury of the elements (1), the thunder crashed and roared. (2) But within the softly lighted library, silence reigned. Presently the door opened and Evelyn DeVere tripped into the room. (3) Gracefully sinking into a chair, she was soon engrossed in the latest novel of the day. (4)

Footsteps were heard (5) and tossing her book aside, (6) Evelyn sprang to meet the newcomer. (7) But disappointment was written plainly on her face when Herbert Vanderslice stepped over the threshold. (8) Although it was not he whom she had expected, she greeted him pleasantly. (9)

The young Vanderslice's nervousness was evident. (10) He paced the floor rapidly for a moment (11), then dropped on his knees at Evelyn's side (12) and clasping her hand in his, cried, "Evelyn, pride of my heart, I love you. I cannot live without you. Say that you will be mine and make me the happiest man in the world." (13)

Evelyn answered, "Herbert, I cannot. I am sorry for your sake that it cannot be, but I do not love you." Withdrawing her hand from his, she rose and, walking over to the table, gazed lovingly at the framed photograph there. (14)

Springing to his feet, (15) Herbert cried, "Ah ha! I see it all now. You love Ralph Grayson — but I swear it now you shall never be his."

Evelyn was greatly frightened by his manner, and her tears fell fast. (16) Turning, Herbert saw Mrs. DeVere standing in the doorway. Giving him a look of scorn, she swept into the room. (17)

"So you would threaten my child — you cad, you scroundel!" she cried. "Leave this house and never darken our doors again." (18) Bewildered at her great wrath, he stood, nailed to the spot. (19) Time passed rapidly (20), still he did not move. Then Evelyn, with never a glance in his direction, took her mother's arm and left the room (21).

"Go!" said Mrs. DeVere. Herbert attempted to speak, but she silenced him with a gesture. Just then the clock struck. (22) Vanderslice staggered through the doorway. Weeks flew by. (23)

It was a beautiful night; the moon rose (24) and its silvery beams played about the room. (25) Mrs. DeVere was sitting in the library, doing a dainty bit of Punchwork, (26) the picture of placid industry, when a hearty laugh was heard, and Ralph Grayson slid into the room. (27)

Dropping her work (28) with a glad cry of welcome, she rose to meet him with outstretched arms (29) "Ralph, my dear boy, I am so glad to see you! When did you return? We have missed you sorely during your travels." (30)

Mrs. DeVere pointed to the conservatory and smiling, said, "You will find her there." (31) Evelyn's mother, memories crowding, sat thoughtfully, but was startled by the sounds of someone creeping softly into the room. (32) Startled to see that it was Herbert Vanderslice, she rose from her chair, and drawing herself to her full majestic height, said in a haughty manner, "Pray, to what do I owe this unexpected intrusion? Have I not forbidden you in the house?" (33)

"Mrs. DeVere, I must and shall see Evelyn, and naught can . . ." Just then the door opened and Evelyn and Ralph danced gaily in (34), smiling and happy. When Evelyn saw Herbert there, she turned a little pale. (35) "Did you wish to see me?" she asked. In the midst of the warmth and light, he shivered, chilled by the frosty tones of her voice, (36) then frowned blackly, and striding toward her, attempted to pass Ralph. But Grayson quickly stepped forward and placed himself as a barrier between them, while Mrs. DeVere whisked her daughter from the room. (37)

Herbert in his great anger strode back and forth tearing his hair. (38) The room seemed intensely hot, and the thermometer rose rapidly. (39) Evelyn, watching the scene from the doorway, caught her breath with fear. (40) Ralph emitted a low whistle (41) as he gazed upon the insane fury of Herbert. Then, hoping to soothe the man, he placed his hand on his shoulder (42), but Herbert turned upon Ralph suddenly and the two grappled in fierce embrace.

Evelyn stood chained to the spot (43), watching the terrific combat, but finally as Ralph threw Herbert to the floor, with a piercing scream (44), she ran to him and fell fainting at his feet. (45)

Herbert slowly picked himself up from the floor and stood quiet and subdued, while they tenderly placed Evelyn in a chair. (46) Mrs. DeVere glared at him and said, "Now, young man, the tables are turned." (47) Evelyn soon revived and gazed scornfully at her rejected suitor. (48) Ralph walked to Herbert with outstretched hands and said, "Vanderslice, take your defeat like a man. I have won Evelyn, and you have lost her, but won't you wish us well?" Herbert stood motionless for a moment, then slowly extended his hand, which Ralph clasped with a hearty grip. (49) Walking to Evelyn, Herbert took her hand, pressed it to his lips, and then, with his face drawn with pain (50), walked haltingly from the room. (51)

Ralph held out his arms, and Evelyn ran into them. Mrs. DeVere laughingly gathered both in her embrace. Presently the lovers sauntered out toward the conservatory. (52) Mrs. DeVere resumed her dainty work, but — affected by the peace and quiet — soon dropped into gentle slumber. (53)

The clock ticked on. The lamp went out. (54)

ACTIONS

1. Branches are waved from behind stage so as to be seen by the audience.
2. Noise made by pan or drums.
3. Actually trips and stumbles.
4. Sprawls in chair and reads comic book.
5. Loud footsteps in uneven time.
6. Throws book high in air over shoulder.
7. Actually jumps.
8. Steps as if over high obstacle.
9. They shake hands. Evelyn goes back to chair.
10. Jerks and acts nervous.
11. Walking as if measuring floor.
12. Drops on knees and acts dramatically.

13. Acts as if talking.
14. Herbert follows Evelyn still on his knees.
15. Jumps up.
16. Squeezed sponge in handkerchief held to her eyes.
17. Sweeps in with broom, places it behind sofa.
18. Points dramatically to door.
19. Hammering offstage.
20. Kid with "TIME" sign runs across stage.
21. Mother holds false arm under real one. Evelyn takes it.
22. Mrs. DeVere strikes Herbert with clock.
23. Mother tears three or four leaves from calendar.
24. Moon (cardboard) is on floor at back. String attached goes over back curtain. Stage hand back of curtain pulls it up.
25. Flashlight.
26. Punches with great force into White Cloth.
27. Slides as if on ice.
28. Drops work, makes noise.
29. Ralph and Mrs. DeVere shake hands.
30. Use red paper heart. Have in back pocket. Look for it first.
31. Mother sits; Ralph exits.
32. Creep in on hands and knees.
33. Both stand up.
34. Evelyn and Ralph waltz in together to center stage.
35. Lifts pail concealed behind sofa, turns it, replaces it.
36. Shivers and blows on hands to warm them.
37. Use whisk broom.
38. Pulls out locks of false hair.
39. Thermometer (large cardboard) pulled up same as moon.
40. Catches with hands.
41. Shrill whistle offstage.
42. Takes left hand with right, places it on Herbert's shoulder.
43. Chains clank. Ralph assists Herbert to lie down on floor.
44. Make any hideous noise offstage.
45. Evelyn slowly and carefully seats herself at Ralph's feet, arranges her dress, fixes hair, then lies on floor.
46. Ralph and Mrs. DeVere lead her to a chair.
47. Ralph and Mother turn end table completely around.
48. Very dramatic!

49. Use briefcase concealed behind sofa.
50. Makes hideous face.
51. Two steps, halt, repeat.
52. Done extravagantly.
53. Loud snores from behind stage.
54. Lamp should be securely fastened to small table on which a long cover, under which a person is concealed, OR table and lamp can be pulled off by means of strong string.

CHAPTER FOUR

CAMPING

CAMP TIME

Most teens complain about having to go to bed *so early* and get up *so early*. By establishing CAMP TIME, you can let them go to bed at 2 a.m. and get up at 9 a.m.! Make the first matter of camp business the establishment of CAMP TIME. Have everyone move his watch *ahead* 2 hours (maybe more or less). All activities will be held according to Camp Time. Even though the teens know about the time change, they really respond to the "new hours." This works most effectively at a week resident camp.

GROUP HUNT

This is a tracking game in which groups try to elude other groups for a period of time in a wooded area, such as a camp. The groups may be tied together with rope so that they must stay together. The idea is for the groups to move quickly and quietly and to work together as a unit. The game may be made as simple or as complex as you want it to be and may be followed with a discussion relating to cooperation and unity.

PARENT-TEEN CAMP

The following retreat idea has been used with great success in establishing a family ministry in the youth program. To attend, there must be at least one teenager and one parent from the same family. The camp begins on Friday, at 9:00 p.m. and ends on Saturday, at 8:30 p.m. This short schedule allows parents to get away and also keeps the cost down.

Schedule

Friday: 9:00 p.m. — All together, Guest Speaker, crowd breakers and surf film.
           10:00 - 10:30 p.m. — Snack time
Saturday: 8:00 a.m. — Breakfast
           9:00 a.m. — Parents — Guest Speaker — Kids — Youth Leader
           10:00 a.m. — Break
           10:30 a.m. — Meet together, Guest Speaker
           11:30 a.m. — Recreation
           12:15 p.m. — Lunch
           1:30 p.m. — Film
           2:00 p.m. — Discussions in groups
           3:00 p.m. — Free time
           5:00 p.m. — Dinner
           6:00 p.m. — Leave for home

The first night, some crowd breakers and a surfing film will help loosen everyone up, especially the parents. You can bring a guest speaker along, who is good with families, to share a short message and spend the rest of the evening just in fellowship. Have fathers room with sons, mothers with daughters, etc. You can work this any way you want. The next day, two meetings are scheduled. The first may be with parents and kids, separated and talked to as individual groups, then everyone meets together in one group for a rap session with the guest speaker. Recreation may include volleyball (Parents must hold hands with their kids — really wild). Basketball can also be a good family game: fathers and guys vs. mothers and gals, but fellows use only one hand. Other games from *Ideas* work well, but include everyone in them. During the afternoon, show the film "Parents, Pressures, and Kids" put out by BFA Educational Media, 2211 Michigan Street, Santa Monica, California. After this, families meet and discuss pressures in their families. It usually takes a while for these to get going, but the results are great. After 45 minutes, the families join together in a large group to share what they felt had been accomplished. Then, discuss ways the families can do things to understand each other better. Kids can share what they like to do with their parents or what they like about their parents and vice-versa. For a short but effective retreat, the long range results of this type of thing can be very good.

SPIRITUAL EMPHASIS CAMPOUT

The following are great ideas for spiritual emphasis campout, or a weekend retreat in a rustic area away from civilization with plenty of natural surroundings:

1. TRUST THE LEADER. Props: Clothesline with knots equally spaced on it. Blindfold everyone except the leader who takes the front of the line. Have EVERYONE take a knot and hold on to it. Complete silence is expected. The leader leads around trees, under bushes, through the swamp, under fences, etc. Object: DISCIPLINE and TRUST THE LEADER TO GUIDE YOU.

2. TREETOP HYMNSING. Pick a large tree with strong limbs. The entire group climbs up the tree and has a treetop hymnsing. Have small chorus books or sheets. Anyone afraid of heights, of course, can sing from the ground underneath the tree.

3. NATURE HIKE. (Purpose: to appreciate God's creation.) Set rules — 1. Everyone remain silent and serious (discipline.) 2. Everyone walk in a line following one another. When one person sees something that is significant about God's creation he shouts "STOP." Everyone huddles around the person while he shares his thought about this thing in God's creation. Some won't have any thoughts to share while others will share more than once.

A.C.T.S. RETREAT

The letters stand for Adoration, Confession, Thanksgiving, and Supplication, which are the four basic ingredients for prayer. It is a retreat primarily geared to a small group of young people who are seriously interested in Bible Study and Prayer.

Source Materials:

Psalms, especially Psalms 95-100. *Prayer — Conversing With God* (Youth Edition), Rosalind Rinker, Zondervan Publishing House, Grand Rapids, Michigan.

After studying Psalms and prayers, many of the young people will be able to write very creative original psalms.

SAMPLE SCHEDULE:

Friday night: Singing, sharing, explain purpose, set the tone for the weekend.

Saturday morning: Group study of ADORATION (praise). Write personal psalms of praise (use Psalm 100 for model if desired).

Saturday afternoon: Discipline of Silence; 3-6 hours or more, depending on desires and maturity of group.

Personal Study of CONFESSION; prepare worksheets or study guides, have devotional books available for reading.

Saturday evening: Sharing, Singing, Group study of THANKSGIVING.

Sunday morning: Group study of SUPPLICATION. Write personal psalms. Discuss results of a consistent prayer life.

COFFEE HOUSE AT CAMP

Very good activity for the final night at camp is to have a coffee house program. At the beginning of the camp, divide the campers into groups of about 7 each. Ask each group to develop a coffee house presentation such as drama, singing, reading, etc. During the coffee house, each group will have the opportunity to make its presentation.

Set up for the coffee house by covering the tables with white paper. If the tables can be folded, place them on the floor in a shape of a circle. Have the campers bring their sleeping bags and blankets to sit or lie upon in front of the tables. Use candles on the tables for light. Have Russian Tea, donuts and popcorn for refreshments. Begin with singing and guitar music. Let each group make its presentation. Close with a time of sharing and prayer.

CHAPTER FIVE

PUBLICITY AND PROMOTION

ABSENCE EXCUSE

The following "Absence Excuse" may be used as an alternative to the old "We missed you last Sunday" postcards. Mail it out with a return envelope and wait for the response.

(Fill out and return in the enclosed envelope immediately!)

Dear Youth Director,

I was absent last Sunday because: (check one)

_____ I was adding up my telephone bill and fainted.

_____ My folks added up my telephone bill and fainted.

_____ My dad strained himself ripping out my phone.

_____ My clothes were in the washing machine.

_____ I was in the washing machine.

_____ My folks were on restriction and I was watching them.

_____ I took out the garbage and they took me by mistake.

_____ My tricycle is in the garage for an overhaul.

_____ I went flying over the weekend and my arms were tired.

_____ I was mugged by an old lady.

_____ I mugged an old lady and spent Sunday in jail.

_____ I don't have a good excuse like those above but I will be there this week to make up for my absence.

Sign Your Name _____

SERIOUSLY: We miss you when you are not with us. Hope to see you at church this week.

POTATO PRINTING

Here is the cheapest and easiest printing your group can do — just for the fun of it or even as a fund-raising project. Here's what you need: (1) some large potatoes cut in half, (2) small knives or razor blades, (3) pencils and paper, (4) scissors, (5) inked stamp pads (the more colors, the better), or a tempora paint soaked sponge. On a piece of paper the size of the flat cut side of a potato, draw a design. (If using numbers or letters, trace it backwards on your potato so it will be forward when printed.) With a knife or felt-tip pen, trace the design onto the flat side of the potato. The portion of the design you cut out of the potato will remain the color of your paper, while the uncut part (or raised portion) of the potato will print the color of ink you choose.

After the design is cut into the potato, press it carefully onto the stamp pad and then onto the paper, making a print. Personalize stationery (of the group or of individuals), membership cards, posters, stickers, etc. Try different colors of ink on top of each other, repeat the design for a border, or stamp a large sheet and cover it with clear contact paper to make a notebook folder, scrapbook cover, or book cover.

(Reprinted with permission from HISWAY, 1445 Boonville, Springfield, Missouri 65802)

SACK MAIL

You can send flat paper bags (lunch type), in the mail. Staple the open end shut and address it on one side and print your message on the other side — or enclose it in the bag. Message Ideas: "Get out of the sack next Sunday morning," or, "This bag can be used to wrap fish — or to invite you to a "rap" session." Or "Blow this bag up and pop it . . . You'll get a bang out of our next event," etc.

CHAPTER SIX

SPECIAL EVENTS

CARHOP FRY OUT

As a fund raiser and special event, have the youth group grill hamburgers, hot dogs, etc., in the parking lot and invite the community to come and eat. The kids serve as "carhops" and wait on people in their cars, taking their orders and bringing the food. Desserts, drinks and other items should be on the "menu" as well.

CRAZY BUS

Divide your busload of kids into teams of no more than 10 (boys and girls). Each team should select a captain who is in charge of organizing the team. Everyone rides on the same bus. Prepare a list of activities each team is going to accomplish. Do not give out the list in advance. Drive to the desired location and then announce what must be done. Points are totaled after each activity.

SOME SUGGESTED ACTIVITIES:

1. BOY DRESS — Go into a neighborhood in your city. Each team is assigned a particular street (or part of a street). Each team will dress a boy as a girl by obtaining different items from homes on their street. Only one item can be received from any one home. The boy best dressed as a girl gains 10 points for his team. The boy then has to wear the costume for the remainder of the evening.

2. BOWLING — Prearrange to use a bowling alley for a short time. Allow each member of the team to bowl one frame. The team having the highest number of pins wins 10 points for the team.

3. EATING CONTEST — Go to a nearby McDonald's. Each team selects a good eater. Buy for each representative of the team two Big Macs, a large order of fries, a chocolate malt and an apple turnover. The one finishing first wins 10 points for his team.

4. FOLLOW THE LEADER — Go to a nearby park. Each team is timed over a course through a kiddie play area (down slide, over sandbox, across monkey bars, etc.). Winning team gets 10 points.

ECOLOGICAL SCAVENGER HUNT

The following is a good activity for get togethers at the beach or at a picnic and park area. Give the kids a list of the following items which must be found *on the ground*. Taking from garbage cans not allowed!! Give points for each item found (no limit per item, that is, someone can bring back 25 aluminium cans and collect 25 points). Also, award bonus points for the most different items on the list. For example, if anyone brings in at least one of every item on the list, he might get a bonus of 100 points. If he brings back 7 different items, 70 bonus points could be awarded, etc. Below is a sample list:

1. Candy wrapper
2. Aluminum beverage can
3. Plastic fork
4. Paper cup
5. Plastic spoon
6. Gum wrapper
7. Paper plate
8. Pop or Beer bottle
9. Napkin
10. Article of clothing

All items must be brought in complete. No tearing things in half and counting them twice. You may add items to the list above as you see fit, depending on where you do it. Give everyone a plastic trash bag to collect their stuff in, and have a prize for the winner.

ECOLOGY WALK

This takes in two ideas and can be very successful if you have a large group of over 25. First of all, as in a regular walk-a-thon, you get sponsors for your kids. Then, as the kids walk, they pick up all the aluminium cans that litter the highways. Have someone follow along and pick up full containers in a truck. Divide the kids in groups of 5 or 6 and send them each in a different direction with plastic bags to be left filled at the side of the road. If you have a good day, you can easily pick up between 500 and 1,000 pounds of aluminum which can be recycled. Cost at present for the cans is somewhere around $200.00 a ton.

FUN FAIR

This activity is good for a whole night's fun and involves creativity, skill and competition. Everyone coming to the evening is told to bring various items such as hammers, nails, string, paper, buckets, etc. They are not told what they are going to do with them. Each person must also bring 50c. As players arrive, they exchange their 50c. for fifty pennies. They are then told to group themselves in teams of two to four people. They have one hour in which to think up and build a games booth for their team.

Various items such as balloons, paper, tacks, etc. may be provided and the participants are allowed to return home for any other needed items. At the end of the hour, the Fun Fair is opened and everyone is free (except the ones left minding the booth) to go round and try the other booths, using up your fifty pennies. Any team is not allowed to try their own booth. The winning team is the one, who after, perhaps an hour and a half, has gained the most money. Examples of booths are a simple penny toss into an ash tray, a dart throwing at a water balloon, a haunted house, a water balloon tossed at an individual, a ball in the bucket, a penny shove, a jail (where you pay one cent to have a friend captured and held in jail for one minute), and even a kissing booth! At one city, this consisted of a series of tables covered with blankets, with an entrance at one end and a voluptuous kisser at the other. Unsuspecting souls paid their money and climbed underneath the tables to find that it was their fate to be kissed by the minister's Labrador Retriever!

GIFT OF LOVE

An effective way for young people to exercise their faith is through helping others without regard for getting anything in return. Try mailing a letter such as the one below to homes in your community and see what develops.

Dear friend,

The members of the church Youth Fellowship want to show appreciation for our special friends by a work day. Can we help you in some way? Does your lawn need mowing? Do you need help getting groceries? Would you want windows washed? Would you like us to read to you? Just visit you?

Just mark on the enclosed card how we can be of some help. If we receive a reply from you, we will come on _____. Please indicate whether you prefer morning or afternoon.

Of course, there is no charge. This is a gift of love.

THE GREAT RACE

Carloads of kids (the same number in each car) leave at the same time, with a list of tasks they must perform. The first team to finish the entire list and return wins the race. Create a list based on your local area and the possibilities it provides. A sample list:

1. Go to the Union Bank Building. Park on the fourth level of their parking lot (if full, wait until a space is available). Everyone go into the bank. One at a time, each member of your team must ride the elevator from the first floor to the 21st floor and back down again.

2. Next, go to Central Park. Everyone take the free tour of the science museum, which is every half hour. The tour lasts 15 minutes. If you just miss it, wait until the next one.

3. Go to Mayor Smith's home at 4352 Birch Street. Everyone sing any Christmas carol you wish, standing on his front porch.

4. Go to Highway 41. Use the trash bag provided and fill it full of litter from along the highway. Do not take cans from any litter barrel along the highway and do not pick up rocks, leaves, etc. Only paper, cans, bottles and other trash.

You can make up other tasks, set a time limit, etc. A sponsor should ride with each group to protect against cheating. The group that finishes most of the tasks in the time limit wins or the first to finish them all wins.

NEWSPAPER NIGHT

The following is a good special event, centered around newspapers. To prepare for it, get a huge pile of old newspapers, the more the better. The following list of games may be played with two or more teams.

1. *Newspaper Costume Race:* Teams have five minutes (or so) to dress kids up with newspaper to look like certain things. For example, Santa and his reindeer, Butch Cassidy and the Sundance Kid, Snow White and the Seven Dwarfs, etc. Tape may be provided each team to help them construct the costumes. Judge for the best job.

2. *Newspaper Treasure Hunt:* Put in each team's pile of papers several specially colored pages and the team to find the most of them in the time limit wins.

3. *Newspaper Scavenger Hunt:* Call out certain items from the papers and the first team to find them wins. For example, a Honda ad, a want-ad for a 1956 Chevy, a news item about a murder, etc.

4. *Wad and Pile:* Teams get ten minutes to wad up all their paper into a big pile. The highest pile wins.

5. *Hide and Seek:* Hide as many kids as possible under the pile of wadded-up papers. The team with the most kids out-of-sight wins. Set a time limit.

6. *Compact Newspapers:* Teams try to compact the paper on their side into the smallest pile possible.

7. *Snow Fight:* Make a line of chairs between the two teams. On a signal, the teams throw all their paper on the other team's side. When time is up (2 or 3 minutes), the team with the least amount of paper on its side wins.

8. *Disposal Event:* Give each team plastic trash bags. The team to get all of the paper in the bags in the fastest time wins.

WANDERLUST

The following may be used as a special event or as a way to open up a good discussion on "purpose and direction in life." Simply follow the instructions below:

1. Have the kids meet at the church, a home, etc., at a pre-advertised time, say 2:00 p.m.

2. Divide the kids into cars, 4 or 5 kids per car. (Make sure you've arranged to have enough cars!)

3. Supply each car with a die (one "dice") and a coin (penny).

4. Announce that this will be a "Wanderlust" experience involving driving around the countryside. Set a finish time (time to stop driving), say 2:45 p.m. Announce that the goal is to see who gets the farthest from the church, house, etc. in 45 minutes (obeying all traffic rules and regulations), WITH THE FOLLOWING CONDITIONS:

5. *Give* the directions (printed on pieces of paper) to each car: "When the signal is given, begin driving your car. You must make a decision at any of these 3 points along the road: (1) 4-way stop sign; (2) traffic light, (3) cloverleaf (interchange). If you come to one of the above points, throw the die. If the die reads 1 or 2, go left; 3 or 4, go straight; 5 or 6, go right. If you come to a dead-end, turn around. If you come to a place where you can't go straight (such as a "T"), then roll the die again. If it comes up an even number go left; if it comes up an odd number, go right. Proceed, driving the car in this fashion until 2:45 p.m. STOP. Record that location as your farthest point."

6. Everyone returns to the originating location at that time and the car that reached the farthest point is the winner. Some will return earlier than others, so have games, refreshments, music or whatever for everyone until the entire group returns.

7. To tie in with a learning experience, the event may be likened to life and how many people do everything by chance. Many just go around in circles, hit dead ends or have no idea what the future holds. Discuss the feelings the group had while on the road and tie in with scripture relating to how Christians receive direction for their lives from God.

SPOOK INSURANCE

Sell "insurance policies" at Halloween to families in the church to protect them against the usual pranks that go along with the ghoulish Holiday. Triple the price for businesses. Since most home owners never need cleanup services, it is clear profit and a good fund raiser. (Make sure you have some kids to do the work in case it *is* needed, however.)

Policy 1: Grass Plat — This policy protects your lawn against such disasters as being strewn with candy wrappers, rocks, rotten eggs and water balloon particles, T.P. (toilet paper), etc.

Policy 2: Diaphanous — This policy will protect your windows against usery — i.e. graffiti, wax, soap, eggs, and other foreign materials. (Does not cover breakage!)

Please fill out the following information.

Name _____ Phone _____

Address _____

Policy 1: GRASS PLAT (Lawn mess)   Price: $ .75 _____

Policy 2: DIAPHANOUS (Window mess)   Price: $ .75 _____

Policy 3: COMBINATION OF 1 and 2   Price: $1.50 _____

Please report claims to the church before 9:00 p.m. on Wednesday, November 3.

ST. PATRICK'S DAY SCAVENGER HUNT

Next St. Patrick's Day, give the following list to teams and give them 45 minutes (or so) to try and collect the following items from around town. Winner is the team with the most green items.

1. Green Lettuce Leaf
2. Green Pear
3. Green Piece of Paper
4. Green Lima Bean
5. Green Stamps
6. Four Leaf Clover or Shamrock
7. Green Garter
8. One Dollar Bill (Silver Certificate)
9. Green Pencil
10. **Green Turtle (Live)**
11. Green Button
12. Green Tennis Shoe (Left Foot)
13. Green Hair Ribbon
14. Bottle of Jade East
15. Green Tooth Pick
16. Green Finger Nail Polish
17. Green Bathing Suit
18. Green Tooth Brush
19. Green Palm Leaf
20. Green Hand Soap
21. Green Straw
22. Green Dixie Cup
23. Green Shoe Lace
24. Green Sweater
25. Green Sucker
26. Green Pickle
27. Green Sock
28. Avocado
29. 7 inch Green String
30. Green Ink
31. Green Balloon — Blown up
32. Green Newspaper
33. Green Flower
34. Green Fish
35. Green Key
36. Green Onion
37. Green Plastic Record
38. Green Book
39. One Pair Green Sun Glasses
40. Green Frog (Live)
41. Green Petticoat
42. Green Lipstick
43. Green Lamp Shade
44. Green Ping-Pong Paddle
45. Green Gum
46. Green Ticket Stub
47. Green Postage Stamp (1c)
48. Jolly Green Giant Picture
49. Green Lime
50. Green Stuffed Animal

PUSHBALL MARATHON

Obtain a giant pushball and plan a day during which your youth will push it all over the community, up and down streets for a distance of from 5 to 25 miles or so. You may have to obtain a parade permit in your city, depending on the conditions, so check this out. Have the kids take pledges from adults to give them so much a mile to push the ball. Pledges may range from 5¢ to $5.00 per mile. The money may be used for a worthy project or charity in the community, and with a little advertising, it can be a very successful service project. Have a car or van with a sign on it lead the way, so that onlookers know what's going on.

BICYCLE CALLING

"Calling" is the ecclesiastical term for visiting folks who have been missing from church for some reason or another. Most church rolls are full of people who are non-participators, many of whom are young people. Rather than making "calling" the youth pastor's job, allow the active kids to do it. One good way is to go out in pairs some Saturday, on bikes. Meet back at the church later, for refreshments and sharing of the day's experiences.

LOVERS SALAD

Next banquet, advertise a "lovers salad." When kids arrive, they will find bowls of lettuce on the table. No celery, tomatoes or dressing — just lettuce. When kids ask about it you tell them that this is the Lovers Salad: "LETTUCE ALONE" . . . get it?

PROJECT DOORKNOB

Distribute flyers around the community announcing that next Saturday (or whenever) your youth group will be passing by in the church bus looking for work to do. If anyone would like some help, simply tie a hankerchief to the front doorknob. As a service project, this work may be offered free to the community. As a fund raiser, you might ask a 50¢ donation (per hour) or something like that. You'll be amazed at how many people will take advantage of this offer.

WORK-A-THON

The idea is to arrange jobs for the kids in the homes of elderly people. These people may be from the church or from the community who cannot afford to pay for the work they need done. The kids then get sponsors who will sponsor them for working in the elderly people's homes, for so much an hour. On the arranged day the kids work an eight-hour day at the different homes, free of charge to the people for whom they are working. Afterwards they can go and collect from each of their sponsors the amount pledged. A date should be set when the money is due. This will make it easier for the kids to collect from their sponsors. One group made over $250.00 with only 10 kids working. One girl in that group made $60.00 for eight hours work. This approach is more effective than Walk-a-Thons or Bike-a-Thons because the sponsors feel they are paying for something constructive and hence are willing to pay more per hour.

BIBLE MARATHON

The *Guiness Book of World Records* has the world record for reading the entire Bible, set at 96 hours by some theological students. Why not try to break it sometime by having kids trade off reading aloud while others listen? The record book just might have your youth's group name in it next year.

BIKE HIKE

Have an all-day outing on bicycles. Plan a route that encompasses 5 to 10 miles out in the country or wherever traffic is light and good riding trails are available. Take sack lunches and have lunch while on the trip. Have the kids wind up at a parking lot or large area where a ''Bike Olympics'' can then be held. These events are good possibilities:

1. *Baton Relay:* Ride bike across the parking lot and hand off baton to next rider on the team.

2. *Slalom Race:* Kids are timed as they ride bikes through a slalom course. Have a stopwatch on hand.

3. *Snail Race:* Mark off a narrow trail and riders must try to stay in the trail and ride as *slowly* as possible. Feet may not touch the ground. The rider with the longest time wins.

4. *Straw Race:* Place coke bottles all over the parking lot with drinking straws in them. Bike riders must ride up to the bottles and pick up the straws with their bare toes, then reach down with their hands and take from their toes.

PHONY CONES

On a hot day trying to keep ice cream from melting is rough. Take a cone and fill it with marshmallows. Then cover with syrup and serve. If you want to go all out, cover with butterscotch and chocolate, sprinkle on some pecans and call it a slow turtle sundae. Another idea is to fill flat bottomed ice cream cones with cake batter and bake. These may be topped with a variety of flavors and do make an interesting addition to an evening. Bake at the temperature and time suggested on the cake recipe. The cone may get a bit soggy but not enough to be any problem.

MISSING PERSON'S PARTY

This event may be done on foot or by using cars. It takes place in a shopping center or business district on a late shopping night when the stores are open. Select 10 to 20 kids to be "missing" in the shopping area. The "victims" have pictures taken in normal dress and those are given to the groups looking for them.

The people who are going to be missing, meet together ahead of time and make up riddles or clues as to the location they'll be in. They also select a disguise appropriate to themselves and the surroundings in which they'll be. For example, kids may disguise themselves as bus drivers, cab drivers, old men, blind men, nuns, pregnant young wives, a man in a wheelchair, repairmen, store clerk, or anything they think they can pull off.

The rest of the group are the "manhunters." They meet at some central location in the shopping area and divide up into groups of from 6 to 10 per group. Each group gets pictures of the victims and the set of riddles and clues in numerical order. Each group is to stick together for the duration of the hunt. When a hunter thinks he has spotted a victim, he approaches the suspected person and says some sort of password like "BEEP BEEP!" If the person is a victim, then he must admit that he has been found. He then tells whether or not there is another missing person with him. If there is another, the hunter informs his group and they continue the hunt. If not, the group goes on after the next victim. The first group to find all its "missing people" wins.

This game works best when you can go in with another youth group and have one group be the "victims" and one group be the "hunters." That way, the kids don't know each other very well, which means they will be harder to find. Also, it gives you more people to participate in the hunt, which makes it more fun. If you have, say, 30 missing people and 30 hunters, then give each hunting group (of 6 per group) 6 missing people to find. Each group hunts for a different bunch of victims. That way you only need one picture of each victim, rather than several (one for each hunting group). Preparation is an obvious requirement of this game. Pictures and disguises must be taken care of well in advance.

You can add another twist to this game by having the hunters "kill" the victims rather than just find them. At the same time, the victims can "kill" the hunters. The killing is done by getting a sticker or piece of tape off the back of the other person. If the victims can kill off more than half the hunting group, then the group has to call off its hunt and is out of the game. However, the hunters have the advantage, so they must "kill" all their victims.

This basic idea may be changed or adapted to meet your own local requirements. It may be called a "Manhunt" or any other name you choose. After the event, meet together to share experiences, have some refreshments and a time for fellowship.

TRUCK-IN

Invite the group to meet at a certain place just before dark. Pile the kids into the back of two or three pick-up trucks (10 to a truck), and take them on a long, slow ride. The more bumps and hills you travel over, the better. The best ride is over the back roads of a farm or through a forest preserve. This could be followed by a picnic, singing and short devotional.

WHITE TREASURE ELEPHANT HUNT AUCTION

This idea combines a treasure hunt, a white elephant sale and an auction. The "treasure" consists of poker chips (or some other form of "play money") which are placed in caches, perhaps 100 locations, in an area around the church property. The area could be much larger, say an entire town, if the group is large and there is enough time and transportation. Each cache may consist of from one to ten chips. A map is made showing the location of the treasure(s) by marking "X." The map may be posted in a prominent location where all can see before the hunt begins. If there are many people involved or if the area is large, make copies of the map for each team. The treasure hunters should work in teams from 3 to 6 persons. At night flashlights are required. At the start, the hunters rush out to the nearest locations, with some crafty ones going to the furthest ones to avoid the crowd. A return time should be set, within 1 to 3 hours, depending on distances. A penalty of 5 white chips per minute late may be assessed. Upon return, the teams can look over the white elephant gifts and other items, which each person brought beforehand. The team members may decide what they wish to bid on, knowing only what the total value of all the chips are. The whites are one, the reds are five and the blues are ten. Then, the auction begins! By offering small items first (then putting them back if there are insufficient bidders at the start) and interspersing them with the more valuable gifts, the excitement can really grow. Having more than one auctioneer is a good idea, too. The auction should last between 15 and 30 minutes. This can be done by offering more than one gift at a time, if necessary.

PERSONALIZED PIZZA PARTY

Provide kids with pizza dough and all the goodies that go on top and let them create their own "personal pizzas." Each person gets a lump of dough and shapes it into a creative design. The only stipulation is that there must be a "lip" so the sauce won't run off. The pizza can be decorated with olives, mushrooms, cheese, pepperoni, anchovies and the like. While these creations are being baked, other games may be played. When they are ready, judge them and award a prize to the most creative pizza. Then eat up!

TURTLE TOURNAMENT

For this special event, you will need to obtain a number of live turtles. Large turtles are best, but the smaller miniature turtles may be used, if the large ones are unavailable. You should have one turtle for every four kids. That constitutes a "turtle team." Turtle events can include the following:

1. *Turtle Decorating Contest:* Provide paint, dye, paper, ribbon, or whatever and have each team decorate its turtle within a given time limit. Judge for the best job and award points.

2. *Turtle Races:* Draw concentric circles on the ground with the largest at about 15 feet in diameter. Place the turtles in the center (the smallest circle) and they may "run" in any direction. The turtle that travels the farthest from the center in the time limit is the winner.

3. *Turtle Tricks:* Each team is given ten minutes to teach, train, or force its turtle to do a "trick." Props may be used and judges should give points for creativity, ingenuity, and whether or not the turtle accomplishes the trick.

4. *Turtle Chariot Races:* Each team is given cardboard, paper, tape, wheels, etc., and they must construct a "chariot" and hook it up to their turtle. Judge for the best chariots and then have a race on a "track" of your choosing.

Keep a tote board with the team names (have each team name their turtles) and their running point total. Have a starting gun, checkered flag, judges wih clip-boards, etc. Provide trophies for the winners and try to create a "derby-day" atmosphere.

CHAPTER SEVEN

CREATIVE COMMUNICATION

GOOD SAMARITAN

The following material may be used to plan a meeting around the parable of the Good Samaritan (Luke 10:25-37). You should familiarize yourself with the parable and get as much background material on Samaritans as possible. Since this is one of the most familiar of the parables, one of the chief objectives of this meeting will be to provide new insights and understanding to details that enrich the story, but which are often lost in the telling. The meeting may include the following exercises:

1. As the group enters, seat all the left handed members (or any other obvious distinguishing characteristics that might make up a minority group) separate from the rest. This should be preferably in the worst chairs, on the floor, behind some obstacle, facing the wrong way, or any other undesirable place. No explanation is needed at this time.

2. Begin with a discussion on "Samaritanism." Use a "concordance" to find 4 or 5 references to Samaritans. Have the group read them, and ask what general attitude toward Samaritans prevailed in New Testament times. Why? Have the group list five or six parallels (contemporary) to this situation. (e.g. Catholics in Northern Ireland, Turkish people on Cyprus, Palestinians in Israel, etc.)

3. Give each person a slip of paper and pencil. Ask the group to write their answers (without signing their names) to this question: In the last six months, have you ever acted like the "priest" or "Levite" in the parable? Then have them pass their papers around. Each person should then silently read the answer he receives. Have the kids share with each other their reactions to this exercise — how they identify with the writer of the answer they received.

4. Ask the group how they feel about the "left-handers," (the "Samaritans") in the room. Did they do anything for them? How do the "Samaritans" feel?

5. Have the class break into groups of four and discuss the two questions, "Who is my neighbor?" and "What does it mean to be a neighbor?" If necessary reread the passage and point out that Christ's response to the first question might help answer the second.

VALUES IN THE CHURCH

The following exercise will help young people (or adults) to set priorities concerning certain values they have and also to see the inconsistencies that often exist within the church community, regarding priorities and values. Print up a 12-square page, such as the one on the facing page and give one to each person. Each square on the page should contain a state of concern.   Have each person cut the twelve squares apart so they have 12 individual concerns on separate slips of paper.

Then follow the steps:

1. Rank them in order of their importance. Put the most urgent or necessary item on top and the least urgent on the bottom. Now, make a list on another sheet from 1 to 12, showing the order you decided on. Put the *letter* of the most important item next to the number 1 and so on through number 12.

2. Now, rank them again, only this time according to the amount of attention they receive in your local church. Put the one receiving the most attention on top, the one receiving the least attention on the bottom. List their letter sequence alongside the first list.

3. Now, compare the two lists. How are they different from each other and why are they different? Should they be the same? What changes need to be made and on which list? Discuss these and other questions you may have with the entire group.

DEATH DRUM

This idea works well in a worship service stressing hunger and starvation in the world. According to statistics (which you may need to update) someone dies of starvation every eight seconds. During the worship service, have someone beat a drum every eight seconds to symbolize another death taking place. The drum interrupting the normal course of the service dramatically illustrates how we often try to ignore the problem of hunger in the world but it just won't go away unless we do something about it.

A Raising Money and Spending it	**B** Developing the music program of the church	**C** Getting workers to fill all the jobs in the church
D Spiritual Growth of church members enabling them to become mature disciples of Christ	**E** Winning local people to Christ	**F** Building and maintaining larger and more attractive church buildings
G Maintaining or building church attendance	**H** Helping to relieve starvation and suffering in the famine stricken areas of the world	**I** Foreign Missionary Work
J Helping to relieve poverty and/or racial prejudice in the local community	**K** Keeping the existing weekly programs of the church going	**L** Developing a sense of fellowship, love and mutual concern

MONITORING YOUR MORALS

The following are true-false questions to be answered individually by the members of the group, then discussed collectively by the entire group. Explain that the answers given should be honest opinion, not answers which might be considered "correct" by the church or youth director. Be prepared to work through each question thoroughly in the discussion period.

1. Over-eating is as wrong as smoking or drinking.

2. While your father was walking home from work one night, a robber came from the shadows and demanded all his money. Your father gave his wallet to the robber. He looked in the wallet and asked, "Is this all the money you have?" Your father said, "Yes." The thief crept away satisfied, but your father had lied to the thief: he had a twenty tucked away in his shirt pocket. This was wrong.

3. To goof off on your job is as wrong as if you stole money from your boss.

4. There are degrees of sin with God and He won't punish us for the little ones.

5. Killing a man is justified when a person is called by his government to defend his country.

6. As Christians, we are to obey all people who are in a position of authority over us. This means police officers, parents, teachers, youth directors, etc.

7. You are late for church so instead of driving at the 45 mile per hour speed limit, you drive at 50. Because you are going to church this is not wrong.

8. Going into your history final, you are just squeezing by with a C. Passing or failing this test could mean the difference between passing or failing this course. There are several questions you don't know, so you look on your neighbor's paper (he is an A student) and copy from him. When you get your paper back you found that you would have flunked without the correct answers from your neighbor's paper. Cheating was justified in this case.

9. You are very much in love with your girl friend and plan to get married. On a date, you get carried away and she gets pregnant. Because you love her as your wife, the act was not wrong.

10. There is a guy at school who really gets on your nerves. If there was ever a person you hated, it would be this guy. The feeling you have for this guy is as wrong as if you killed him.

NEWSSTAND

Listed below are thirty popular magazines found on most newsstands. They reflect a wide range of interests. There are many others, of course, and you may want to add or subtract titles from the list before using it.

1. Rolling Stone
2. T.V. Guide
3. Ladies Home Journal
4. Holiday
5. Psychology Today
6. Surfer
7. Time
8. Playboy
9. Seventeen
10. Sports Illustrated
11. Readers' Digest
12. Mad
13. Hot Rod
14. Intellectual Digest
15. U. S. News & World Report
16. Better Homes and Gardens
17. Parents
18. Playgirl
19. Esquire
20. Police Gazette
21. Consumer Reports
22. Ms.
23. Wall Street Journal
24. Glamour
25. National Geographic
26. Hollywood Reporter
27. Decision
28. Ramparts
29. National Enquirer
30. People

Divide into small discussion groups of not more than 8 each (4 to 6 in a group is usually best). Try to avoid "cliques" getting together into the same group. Perhaps a random method of selecting groups might help. Print copies of the above list and distribute to each person. The three questions below are asked one at a time and each person is allowed to share his or her response with the others in the discussion group. Anyone may pass if they wish.

1. Which magazine(s) best describes you right now? Explain why.
   Which magazine(s) best describes the way you would like to be?

2. Due to a sudden paper shortage, the government will only permit three magazines to continue being published. Those three magazines are to be determined by a vote of the people. Which ones will you vote for?

3. If you had one full page in any magazine to do with as you wish, how would you use it? What would be printed on the page, and in what magazine would it appear?

Allow ample time after each question for everyone to respond. Remember that in a discussion such as this, there are no "correct" answers. The important thing is that everyone has the opportunity to express himself openly and honestly, which invariably leads to more openness, better understanding and communication among the members of the group. You may want to "wrap up" the experience, however, with a challenge or lesson that gives added content. Question one is an introductory or self-analysis type of question. Question two deals with values and priorities, and question three with communication. Any of these topics may be discussed. Further application is left up to you and your objectives.

TIME MACHINE

The following story and exercise may be used most effectively with kids to help them to determine the worth of man and his values. It also forces a group to work something out together and come to a group decision. To begin, tell the following story:

"There is about to be a nuclear holocaust. The human race as we know it will be totally wiped out. However, ten people have discovered a way to survive by getting into a time machine, which will take them into the future and they may at that time start the human race all over again. The ten people are:

1. An accountant
2. His pregnant wife

3. A liberal arts coed
4. A pro-basketball player

5. An intelligent female movie star
6. A black medical student
7. A famous novelist
8. A bio-chemist
9. A 70-year old clergyman
10. An armed policeman

Unfortunately, at the last minute, it is discovered that the machine will only take six people instead of the original ten. Your job, as a group, is to decide which six will be saved and which four must die. You have 30 minutes in which to decide."

Have the kids work this out in small groups of 4 or 5, then at the end of the time period, share their conclusions with the entire group. Have the kids disregard the technicalities of the story, but to concentrate on the process of arriving at a decision based on the facts given. After each group shares its selections, ask questions for further discussion, like: How did your group get along during the process of making a decision? Did you listen to each other or were you so stubborn that no progress was made? Did you feel that no one would listen to you? Did you feel that you had the right answers? Are there in fact any right answers? What do your selections teach you about your values?

Editor's note: Similar exercises can be found in the book *Values Clarification* by Sidney Simon, published by Hart Publshing, New York

TEN STEPS TO ACTION

It is one thing to see problems in the world and another thing to do something about them. As an exercise to help kids to see what they can do, give the following instructions, one at a time and give enough time for kids to think through each point. Discussion can follow.

1. List 5 social problems in your community.
2. Circle 3 for church.
3. Underline 2 of those you can do.
4. Rewrite one of these 2.
5. List 5 things to be done to deal with this problem.
6. Circle 2 you can do.
7. Underline 1 you can do.
8. What will hinder you from accomplishing the task?
9. What will help you to do it?
10. Will you do it?

REAL WORLD GAME

The following simulation game may be used effectively prior to a discussion on poverty in the world, selfishness, war, international relations, or any number of relevant subjects. The game requires about an hour and a half and involves a somewhat realistic situation of survival centering around the grain production and needs of various countries. The game involves 7 groups of 6 to 10 persons (it may be adapted to a different number of groups) with each group becoming a country with designated grain production and grain needs per month and also a monthly income.

Materials needed:
  a) Fifteen plus cups grain (unpopped popcorn or whatever may be conveniently measured and handled).
  b) Three rolls of pennies (the income could be changed to dollars so play money could be used).
  c) Eight plastic measuring cups with graduations to ⅛ th cup. The leader gets a cup and each country gets one cup.
  d) Seven, 3 x 5 "weather" cards with three of them having instructions (see 3c under World Situation Fact Sheet).
  e) Eight copies of the World Situation Fact Sheet — one for the leader and one for each country.

Procedure:

Most of the instructions are included on the World Situation Fact Sheet. However, the leader needs to keep a few other things in mind:
  a) To save confusion, have all the supplies distributed to each team before the "preparation" period begins.
  b) Make sure all the taking of the monthly consumptions and giving of monthly production and income is fully completed between each monthly time period before another time period is begun.
  c) Between each time period collect the "weather" cards and reshuffle them and have the presidents pick them randomly. This too, should be done before a new time period is begun.
  d) It is important that the leader refrain as much as possible from giving additional instructions or answering questions, etc., once the game is in process. This will allow for more initiative by the players in tackling the task without constantly depending on the leader to guide toward a successful conclusion.

If your situation calls for a different number of countries than 7, then you will need to make a new World Situation Fact Sheet. In setting up a different situation, make sure the total production of all the countries is slightly more than the total needed. This will allow (at least theoretically) survival of every country.

World Situation Fact Sheet

Country	*Direct Trading Countries	Monthly Grain Production	Monthly Grain Needs	Monthly Gross National Income
Canada	All Countries	2 Cups	½ Cup	$ .03
China	Japan, Great Britain, Canada ONLY	2½ Cups	3 Cups	.01
Great Britain	all but Russia	½ Cup	¾ Cup	.03
India	all but China	¾ Cup	2 Cups	.01
Japan	all but Russia	¼ Cup	1 Cup	.04
Russia	India, Canada, United States ONLY	2½ Cups	1½ Cups	.02
United States	all but China	2½ Cups	1¼ Cups	.05

*Trading with countries that you're not allowed to trade with DIRECTLY, MAY be traded with through a neutral country acting as an intermediary. A neutral country is one that can trade directly with the countries who want to negotiate.

Instructions

1. GOAL: Your purpose is to survive as a nation in whatever way you choose: beg (foreign aid), borrow, buy, (or steal!)

2. PREPARATION: You will have 10 minutes in which to study the fact sheet and elect the following officers:

   a) President — to lead in deciding his country's policy and to negotiate with other countries who come to him. He MAY NOT leave his own country.

   b) Ambassador — to negotiate for his country in other countries. You may elect more than one ambassador if you feel the need.

   c) Treasurer — to keep track of and guard the grain and money.

3. METHOD OF PLAY:

   a) The game is played in time periods of one month, 6 months total, of 10 minutes each month. Each month you will receive your monthly income and grain quotas. At the end of each month, you will have taken away from your monthly consumption of grain. Your job is to see that, in the 10 minutes allotted, you have enough grain at the end of the month to equal the consumption to be taken away.

b) When time is called at the end of each month, all play must stop; and all inter-country communication must cease; and all players must return to their respective countries.

c) At the beginning of each month, except the first, each country's president will draw a weather card; a clear card indicates good weather and no change in grain production; "FLOODS" and "DROUGHT" cards mean your grain production is cut in half that month, "BUMPER CROP" means you have 1 cup extra (large grain producers) or ½ cup extra (small grain producers) that month.

4. STARVATION:

If you haven't enough grain at the end of any monthly time period to meet your needs, your country starves and is out of the game.

PROBLEM LETTER

Most youth leaders who have any rapport at all with kids receive numerous requests for help. These requests are a valuable resource for intragroup, youth-to-youth ministry. Take such a request, or any of your own choosing, and put it in the form of a letter. Mimeograph it and present it to the youth group for their answers.

If the case is an actual one, take care to fictionalize it just enough to hide the identity of the person seeking help. You don't want kids playing a guessing game as to who the "mystery person" is. That kind of thing could be disastrous. You should make every effort to protect against revealing the identity of any actual person(s) involved.

After the letter is presented to the group, it may be read aloud and the problems discussed, seeking some answers to resolve the issues presented. One approach might be to break into small groups to work on answers. The leader must take care to insure the answers that arise apply to the problems and also that the group is not just swapping ignorance — not just a lot of head knowledge or advice-giving. The key is the type of questions the leader may ask. For example, "Why do you think that?" or "How would Christ respond?" Also emphasize the practical by asking, "What things have you found to work in such situations?" Be careful to stimulate up-to-date and down-to-earth, meaningful responses.

The following letter is a sample of one used before. You may use it as a guide for writing your own, or you might choose to use this letter as it stands. Of course, such a letter may deal with many other problems than the ones contained in this sample.

It should appear to be as "real" as possible. That way kids are more serious about helping out with some good advice. You might even want to give some background information on the person who wrote the letter, again without revealing anything that would tip off kids as to "who" it is.

Dear Alvie,

How are you doing? You know I have been having problems at home and I value your opinion more than anyone else's I know. I know that if I give you a problem to solve or whatever, I know you can take it and look at it objectively. I think that is real good.

Well first of all, my parents tend to put their beliefs, convictions, or whatever on me. Now I realize they have experienced some things I haven't and that I never may, but I feel that they are sheltering me too much. For example, no guy is allowed over here if they aren't here at home. This right here insults me and also hurts me (let alone annoys me). It insults me because it implies they don't have faith in the type of people I choose for friends. Whenever I ask them about it, they always say, "What will people say?" or "What will the neighbors think?" or else "We are only trying to protect you from a bad situation." Those are exact quotes.

Now, I understand I am their daughter and that they are responsible for me but why do they have to carry it so far? I'd like to know what they are going to do in a year when I have my own apartment and I can do whatever I please (to a certain extent).

People tell me to grin and bear it a year longer but I live right now, not in the future and I don't care to live under such circumstances. I'm not saying I don't have freedom because I have some — like I drive the car to school every day, but Dad uses that as a string to get me to do what he wants. It's like a threat every time I don't comply with what he wants.

I guess what I am asking for is advice on how I can think for myself and not have to be protected. One of the latest things that happened was this Sunday. I told them they didn't have to worry about trusting me, because I didn't ever try to cover up anything from them. I told them that I have smoked and drank and smoked dope. Then they thought I was some sinner and that I needed to become closer to God. They kept me up 'till about twelve preaching at me and telling me how bad and how wrong I was.

First of all, I'll tell you my feeling on smoking, etc. I think smoking cigarettes is bad for a person and it is a habit I hope I never have and, no, I don't smoke. I've tried it and I didn't think it was too cool.

I drink every now and then and I don't feel it is wrong for me. What I think would be wrong is for me to get drunk. That is one thing I just don't dig and I can't see it — having a hangover and everything else that goes along with it.

I guess you could call me a social drinker. I'll have a beer of whatever if I am out with kids but I very seldom do — like maybe one or two times a month. In essence, I feel drinking is fine with moderation. But what about reputation?

Smoking dope is a constant front to me. Kids are always doing it and I say no. I've smoked it more than once but it didn't affect me. It was just like smoking hot air. The last time I did was last summer and I haven't since. I don't know if grass is right or wrong. That is just one thing I can't decide on. I don't really care, because if I want to smoke it I can and if I don't want to, then I won't. I'm not planning on it. It doesn't turn me on — neither does it turn me off.

Alvie, what I wish you would do is give me your views on the three previous things and also give me some advice on how I can get along better with my parents.

You are probably wondering about my Christian life. Well, I know God is there and if I want Him I can get Him. I try to read my Bible in the morning and at night sometimes. I fail because I am tired or hurried. Praying is a struggle for me, because I have not found any effective way to communicate with God and Christ. Sometimes I wonder if I love God. I know the Bible says, "If you love me, you will keep my commandments." But what are they? I really would like to have a personal relationship with God but I am not sure how and if I did know how, I don't know if I would be willing to put out the effort. Maybe you could advise on this also. I would appreciate it greatly.

Well, I guess the last topic of discussion is Steve. He comes and sees me every Saturday. This weekend he is taking me down to Junction City to meet his parents. I really like him a lot, possibly love more than just a friend. I don't want to end this relationship ever and neither does he. It's a type of agreement between Steve and me. I *someday* want to marry him if things work out the way they have been. Both of us feel the same way about it and we are willing to wait for things to work out the way that is best, which wouldn't be until after we both graduate this year. If you would, please pray that I can be open minded about this and will do what is best from God's point of view.

I hope this letter hasn't been too exhausting. If you could, please answer me promptly. I realize you have other things to do besides answer letters but I would be happy if you could just show this some special thought and consideration. However, I will understand if you can't because you are so busy. Thanks for your time and trouble. Hope to hear from you soon.

Your friend,

Jan

GRAVEN IMAGES

Read the second commandment given to Moses to your group or study together the story of the golden calf which followed the receiving of the Ten Commandments. Then give each youth the necessary materials to sculpture a modern day "image" out of balsa wood or clay. The sculptured images may be realistic or symbolic, but should represent things young people often put before God. A discussion may follow, with each person sharing his image and the images can further be dedicated to God by their destruction. For example, the wooden ones could be burned or the clay ones could be heaped together and remolded into a symbol of the Faith.

LETTER TO AMOS

The following is good after a study of the Old Testament book of Amos. Pass out copies of this "open letter" to Amos and discuss the arguments presented. Some suggested questions for discussion follow:

Dear Mr. Amos,

Your intemperate criticisms of the merchants of Bethel show that you have little understanding of the operations of a modern business economy. You appear not to understand that a businessman is entitled to a profit. A cobbler sells shoes to make money, as much as he can. A banker lends money to get a return on his loan. These are not charitable enterprises. Without profits a tradesman cannot stay in business.

Your slanders reveal also a lack of appreciation for the many contributions made to our land by the business community. Visitors to Israel are greatly impressed by the progress made in the past few decades. The beautiful public buildings and private homes are a proud monument. Increasing contacts with foreign lands add to the cultural opportunities open to our citizens. Our military strength makes us the envy of peoples already swallowed up by her enemies.

Despite the great gains during Jereboam II's reign, there is some poverty. That we admit. But is it just to blame us for the inability of some people to compete? You say that the peasants were cheated out of their lands. Not so! They sold their property. Or in some cases, it was sold for back taxes. Some peasants put up the land as collateral on a loan, then failed to meet the payments. No one was cheated. The transactions to which you refer were entirely legal. Had you taken the trouble to investigate the facts, your conclusions would have been more accurate.

The real reason for poverty is lack of initiative. People who get ahead in this world work hard, take risks, overcome obstacles. Dedication and determination are the keys to success. Opportunities don't knock, they are created by imagination and industry.

Our success can be an inspiration to the poor. If we can make it, they can too. With the growth of business, Israel grows. More jobs, better pay and increased opportunity for everyone. The old saying contains more than a germ of truth; What's good for General Chariots is good for the country.

Yours for Israel.

Discussion Questions:

1. Evaluate the merchant's arguments in light of justice. At what points do the businessmen convince or fail to convince you?

2. Suppose this letter were written today — how would you react? Where do the rights of the individual stop? Can justice be administered without striking a balance between individual rights and rights of the community?

3. What about Justice, Just Us or Just U.S.??????

DON'T TALK WITH YOUR MOUTH FULL

In most of our affluent churches, a discussion with youth on "food and fasting" may be very worthwhile. Such a discussion may be wrapped around a study of biblical fasts to determine the relevance or need for fasting today. Below are a few quotes, references and discussion questions to stimulate interest in the topic.

Quotes:

1. "Food is not the most basic essential in life. The greatest bodily need is Air. The second is not food, but Water. Third is not food, but Sleep! Food comes *fourth* but in thousands of Christians' lives, it seems to be put first. Too much food clogs the system. To over-eat is a sin of waste and a *sin against the body*, shortening the physical life and dulling the spiritual. If you are not its *master*, you are its slave!" *Winkie Pratney*

2. "The appetite for food is perhaps more frequently than any other the cause for backsliding and powerlessness in the church today. God's command is 'whether you *eat* or *drink*, or whatsoever you do, do all to the glory of God.' Christians forget this and eat and drink to please *themselves*. They consult their appetites instead of the laws of life and health. More persons are snared by their tables than the church is aware of. A great many people who avoid alcohol altogether will drink tea and coffee that in both quality and quantity violate every law of life and health. Show me a gluttonous professor and I will show you a backslider." *Charles Finney*

3. "It is important for us to distinguish between a desire or appetite for food and a hunger for food. It is doubtful whether the average individual, reared in our well-fed Western civilization, knows much of genuine hunger. The sensation of emptiness or weakness, gnawing in the pit of the stomach and other symptoms experienced at the outset of a fast are seldom real hunger. They are a craving for food resulting from the long-continued habit of feeding ourselves three times a day without intermission for three hundred and sixty-five days a year." *Arthur Wallis*

Discussion Questions:

1. How do you react to Finney's statement? Why?

2. What do you think Finney meant when he used the phrase "the appetite for food"?

3. How could Finney link the idea of "powerlessness in the church" with the "appetite for food"? Do you think it is valid?

4. How is it possible to eat to the glory of God?

5. How much gluttony does it take to make one gluttonous?

6. What is your definition of fasting?

7. Is fasting a valid form of worship for people today? Why?

References:

1. The Bible, God

2. Buchinger, Otto H. F., *About Fasting — A Royal Road to Healing;* Thorsons Publishers Ltd.

3. Ehret, Arnold, *Rational Fasting:* Ehret Literature Publishing Co., Beaumont, Cal. 92223

4. McMillen, S.I., *None of These Diseases:* Spire Books, Fleming H. Revell Co., Old Tappan, N.J.

5. Shelton, Herbert M., *Fasting Can Save Your Life:* Natural Hygiene Press, Inc.

6. Wallis, Arthur, *God's Chosen Fast:* Christian Literature Crusade, Fort Washington, Pennsylvania.

COMMUNION ON CANVAS

For a truly unique approach to the Communion service hang a giant canvas (butcher paper will do) in the front of your meeting room, large enough for everyone participating to draw a small "painting" upon. Set up a table with the wine and bread on one end, and with paints, paste, pictures, etc. on the other. After some singing, read appropriate Scripture from a modern translation. The leader then without further words, goes to the canvas and draws a picture, then partakes of the communion elements. (His picture may be anything he wishes, perhaps only words.) The second person does the same and then the leader serves the second person with the elements saying, "This is the blood of the Lord which was shed for you. This is the body of the Lord, broken for you . . ." The second person serves the third, and so on. The result will in all probability be a magnificent painting depicting the group's beliefs and hopes, and an unusually beautiful worship experience.

PERFECT PAIR

For a good discussion on the family, and as a way to discover the values of kids in the group, try this. Simply tell kids they are to find the world's most perfect couple, that is, the man and woman best suited to create the ideal home and family, and most likely to be happy. Divide into small groups and have them describe their perfect couple. Things to consider:

1. The couple themselves
   a. background
   b. age
   c. education
   d. religious affiliation
   e. race
   f. political views

2. Their lifestyle
   a. jobs (employment)
   b. hobbies
   c. sex life
   d. leisure time
   e. entertainment
   f. habits
   g. friends and associations

3. Their possessions
   a. money
   b. furniture
   c. house and neighborhood
   d. books, magazines
   e. appliances
   f. recreational needs
   g. auto(s)

4. Philosophy on child rearing
   a. discipline
   b. education
   c. manners
   d. dress
   e. independence

The items listed are only suggestions and kids should not be limited to them. After a 20- or 30-minute period of working in the groups, have each describe their perfect couple. Make lists on the blackboard or on an overhead projector. Compare each group's description of its couple. Discuss the differences and similarities and ask *why* certain characteristics were selected. Talk about prejudices and relate to scripture. How does God describe His perfect family? What matters and what doesn't? Also discuss the interaction that took place in each small group. The disputes, differences of opinion, prejudices, etc. You can get hours of healthy discussion out of this exercise.

PEOPLE PUZZLE GROUPS

The following is an experiment in communications. First divide your large group up into smaller groups of five. (Pick helpers if there are people left over — the ones you think would get the least out of the experiment.) Each group of five gets an envelope with different shapes of the same color in it for each member. Use construction paper to make shapes out of these colors: Red, Blue, Black, Yellow, Green. Each person's envelope contains shapes in one of these colors. The object is to form five rectangles, all of equal length and width. However, you cannot speak. You will need pieces from the other envelopes and others will need your pieces. There are three steps in putting together the puzzles:

1. No speaking. The only thing you can do is offer one of your pieces of the puzzle to another member. You cannot indicate your need for a particular piece. You may only take a piece if it is offered to you. (5-10 minutes)

2. No speaking. However, you can now indicate your need for a particular puzzle piece. (5-10 minutes)

3. You may speak.

4. (optional) You may help another group finish.

This exercise usually takes from 20-30 minutes for all the different groups to finish. The discussion follow-up must be based on the interaction during the experiment. Discussion takes place in the areas of communication and competition, drawing quickly to human feelings. That's the important thing — how did you feel:

a. When you couldn't talk? Did others help you? Why was communication in your group hard (or easy)?

b. About the others in your group? Were they selfish or generous? Do you consider yourself generous or selfish?

c. When your group finished? Were you proud? When did you start competing with other groups? (This always happens, but never use the word team or competition, always groups and experiment.)

d. When another group wanted to help you? Did you like the other groups or feel they were showing off, etc? Which was the best group? The worst group? Why?

e. How did you feel about yourself, your motives? How do you feel about your ability to communicate? Man's ability to communicate?

You can see the different avenues open up, and you must be able to take advantage of them. You could end up in a discussion of God's communication to man, why it is so difficult — why He had to become a man to communicate! Or you could end up in other directions — man's selfishness, pride, competitive nature, etc. Base it on the interaction of your particular group.

HOW TO MAKE THE PUZZLES

When each group has finished, you will have the five rectangles made by piecing the colors together as follows:

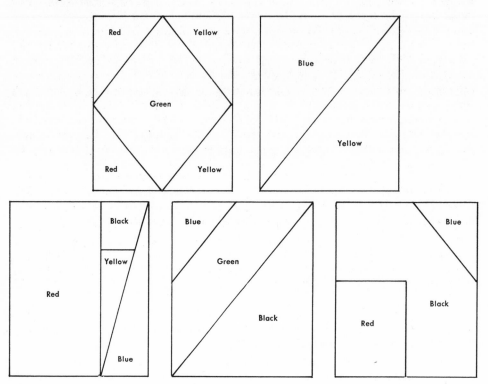

To prepare envelopes, cut the above shapes from the designated colors of construction paper. Make sure they form the five rectangles. Then put all the reds in one envelope, all the blues in another, etc. These five envelopes make up enough for *one* group. If you have five groups, you need 25 envelopes, divided so that each of five groups can complete the puzzle and each of the five people in that group have a different color.

BALLOON WORSHIP

Pass out balloons and small slips of paper as the group assembles. As a *Call To Worship*, ask everyone to write on the slip the nicest thing he can say about someone else. "I love you," "I think you're great" — "You turn me on," etc. Then ask that they roll up the slips and place them inside the balloons and blow the balloons up and tie them. Hold them as the service progresses and as an *Offering*, have everyone bat the balloons forward over each other's head to the altar or worship leader. The "messages" become our offering to God. At the end of the service, ask the group to come to the front and grab a balloon, any balloon and POP IT. The message they receive from the balloon is the *Benediction* to the service, a message to us from God. Note: sometimes in the melee at the end, some balloons might be accidentally broken, so some people might not get one. It would be a good idea, then, to have some sponsors make two or three extra to have at the front. This could also be used in connection with some of the creative worship ideas in *Catch the New Wind,* published by Word, Inc.

INTER-CHURCH ESPIONAGE

The following is a simulation game designed to teach the internal unity among true members of the Body of Christ. The game is set up as a fun thing, the players being unaware that the game has been rigged to teach a profound truth. Although the game's instructions are somewhat elaborate, this is only to disguise the simplicity of the game. Here's how it works.

A. Before the game:

    1. Prepare enough slips of paper to enable everyone in the crowd to have one. Select about four sets of numbers, such as:

53	121	207	129
219	107	21	101
21	49	119	47
107	123	53	123

        Fold the papers and shuffle them so they are all mixed up. The important thing is that all the number sets add up to the same sum. (In this case, 400) The players are unaware of this, of course.

    2. Get enough pennies for everyone to have one. Part of the game involves flipping coins.

3. Also have golf pencils on hand for everyone who needs one.

B. Explain the game to the crowd as follows:

1. You are all spies. In a moment you will receive a slip of paper with numbers on it. By adding the numbers, you will know the code number of the country you are spying for. The person next to you could be an enemy spy or he might be a friend from your country. You don't know. Don't reveal your code number until you have to, and make sure you add the numbers correctly.

2. The object of the game is to: (a) eliminate enemy spies from the game, (b) locate and team up with your fellow spies and (c) avoid being eliminated from the game. In other words, whichever country survives without being eliminated is the winner.

3. You will also receive a coin and a pencil with your code number. When the game begins, add up your numbers and write the total on the paper. Next, go up to any person in the room. One of you calls "Odd," one "Even." Flip your coins. If they both turn up the same, whoever called "Even" is the "aggressor" and the other person is the "responder." If, when flipped, the two coins turn up different (one heads and one tails) whoever called, "Odd" becomes the aggressor.

4. After you determine who the aggressor is, the aggressor asks, "Friend or foe?" The responder must then show his code number.

   a. If it is the same as the aggressor's the responder remains in the game because he is a friendly spy and on the same team. He now joins the aggressor by holding on to his waist and following behind.

   b. If the responder's code number is different from the aggressor's the responder is out of the game.

5. At this point, if you are still in the game, you find other survivors and the process is repeated. If you have a fellow spy behind you, then you work as a group. You are the spokesman for the group, however, if you were the original aggressor. You approach another individual or group, flip coins (per instruction 3) and you will either eliminate, be eliminated, or form a larger group.

6. Keep this procedure going until only one group is left. This will be the winning country.

C. Play the Game.

1. Make sure there is enough room for the snake-like groups to form and move

about. Of course, as the game progresses, no one will be eliminated, and all will be absorbed into one long group.

2. Try to keep the game going. The players will eventually realize there aren't any enemy spies before the game is completely over. It doesn't take long for the game to be played.

D. Discuss

1. What did you assume about the game that wasn't true? (That there were different countries, when actually there was only one.)

2. If you had known ahead of time there weren't any enemy spies how would it have affected your play? (Probably wouldn't have been threatened, therefore, no need to compete or be suspicious of others.)

E. Application

1. We are all members of the same team, but often we forget and are threatened by the unknown responses of others.

2. As Christians we are all members of one Body (1 Cor. 12), yet we have fractured it on all levels (denominations, cliques).

3. On a broader scale, we are all members of the family of man. We should seek to understand others better and learn to live in harmony.

WHAT'S NUMBER ONE?

These questions are to be answered by each individual on a sheet of paper, then followed up by discussion:

1. What's your favorite magazine?

2. If you could be anyone else, who would you be?

3. When you daydream, what are you doing?

4. If you could buy anything, what would you buy?

5. When you picture yourself doing something "cool and neat" (mental act of heroism), what are you doing?

6. When you see a person of the opposite sex, how do you picture this person in relationship to yourself?

7. When you see a person of the same sex, how do you picture this person in relationship to yourself?

8. What would you like to do for your life's work?

9. What's good about you? (Don't be humble!)

10. If you could change anything about you, what would you change?

Observations:

A. These questions show quite clearly what the most important thing in a person's life is.

B. Complete involvement of an individual in one specific area of life is abnormal. The activity becomes distorted. It is not that important.

C. Matthew 6:33 — discussion.

D. Questions 9 and 10 show a person's "self-concept." God loves each one of *as we are*, and He can use us *as we are* (Physical build, etc.). We don't need to be heroes to be useful in His sight.

HEARING AND SEEING GAME

The following instructions should be copied and given to each player:

Get into groups of three. Listen to the SOUNDS OF SILENCE. Read to yourself Matthew 13:10-16. Read the lyrics of the song.

Your group is composed of three people. Each of you will eventually do the following "jobs" . . . :

(1) COMMUNICATOR: Your job will be to tell the other two members of your group your responses about the questions below. Be honest. If you don't like the questions, form new ones to which you can respond.

QUESTIONS: What are your immediate feelings about the song? What is its central point? What is it saying about communication? Do you see any relationship between the song and the scripture verses? How can we really understand each other? In what ways can you improve communication in class? At home? At school? In town?

(2) INTERVIEWER: You should try to help the "Communicator" in what he or she is trying to say. Ask questions related to the questions above. If you see something in the background of what he is saying that might be important, bring it out, ask him about it. Help clarify and develop the meaning of what he's saying.

(3) RECORDER: Listen very carefully to the interview. Take notes on the entire discussion. Make lists of important words or phrases. Try to be a good listener. Be ready to report to the larger group when it reconvenes.

This process is composed of three periods of 5-6 minutes each. You will rotate "jobs" as follows:

Period One: "A" is the Communicator; "B" is the Interviewer; "C" is the Recorder

Period Two: "A" is the Recorder; "B" is the Communicator; "C" is the Interviewer

Period Three: "A" is the Interviewer; "B" is the Recorder; "C" is the Communicator

After all have finished, ask for the Recorders to report on what they heard. List major ideas. Reread the scripture passage. As follow through, you may want to assign group projects based on the ideas and probes presented. (SOUNDS OF SILENCE was recorded by Simon and Garfunkel, Columbia Records #CL2469). Any other popular song may be used as well.

YOUTH GROUP COAT OF ARMS

Have each young person draw a "Coat of Arms" emblem similar to the one below, with six compartments. (Any shape or size.)

In each of the six spaces have the kids draw the following with paints, pens, felt tips, or whatever they want:

1. Symbolize something our youth group has done for others in the past.
2. Symbolize the purpose of our youth group.
3. Draw what you think the most important activity of our youth group is.
4. Draw a picture of our youth group's greatest achievement last year.
5. Symbolize what you feel the goal of our group should be.
6. Include three words that should be most important to our group.

This can be a good exercise for allowing your youth to expressively voice their feelings about the group, plus you might get a few good emblems as well.

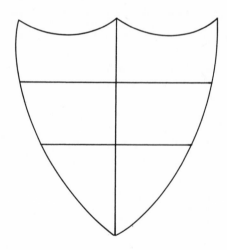

BODY LIFE GAME

This game is a good way to demonstrate the need for cooperation and unity within the Body of Christ as presented in New Testament Scripture. To set up the game, divide the entire group into five smaller groups, which will symbolize various members or parts of the body. Each group should be named accordingly, i.e., EYES, HANDS, EARS, FEET and MOUTH.

The object of the game is fairly simple. The five groups, all members of the same body, must work together to perform various tasks before LIFE dies. To symbolize LIFE, someone may be locked in a trunk or box and a road flare lit nearby. When the flare goes out, LIFE will be considered dead. The only way LIFE can be saved is to complete the tasks which leads to the trunk key and lets LIFE out before the flare burns out. (Flares are usually good for about 30 minutes.)

EYES	HANDS	EARS	FEET	MOUTH

Each of the five groups (EARS, HANDS, EYES, FEET, MOUTH) should be equal in size and labeled in some way (Different color arm bands or signs hanging around their necks, etc.). To complete the tasks, each group may function in only the way it functions in a normal body. In other words, an EYE will not be able to hear and an EAR won't be able to see. EYES can only see and EARS can only hear. Therefore, everyone except the EYES must be blindfolded.

When the game begins, the blindfolds go on, the flare is lit and the group gets its first task. The instruction for that task is written and presented to the EYES, who whisper it to the EARS, who likewise whisper it to the MOUTHS, who then verbalize it to the rest of the body. Whenever the group must go anywhere, the FEET must carry the EYES (the only ones who can see) and the remaining members of the body must follow behind in a single file line, holding on to each other's waists. The EYES in that case are allowed to speak, giving directions to the rest of the body.

The tasks may be relatively simple ones. Three or four good ones are enough. A few examples are listed below:

1. Crackers and juice should be fed to the MOUTHS by the HANDS while being guided by the EYES. The FEET will then carry the EARS to (place) followed by the rest of the body in single file.

2. The EARS will be given a number (by the leader) between one and ten. The EARS must then hold up that many fingers for the EYES to see, who then tell the MOUTHS, who shout it to the HANDS and FEET. Everyone must then get in smaller groups of that number of people. The EYES may help everyone get together. (This can be repeated.)

3. Splints and bandages may be provided which the HANDS should use to splint one arm and one leg of each of the FEET, guided by the EYES.

The above tasks are only samples. It is best to work out a few things your group can do to fit each local situation. The last task should lead to the envelope which contains the key to the trunk. The HANDS must use the key to open the trunk, again guided by the EYES and carried there by the FEET.

The discussion which follows could include the following questions:

1. Talk about the game and how each part of the body did or did not function.

2. Did everyone do his part?

3. Why didn't some people get involved?

4. Relate this to Paul's analogy of the body (1 Corinthians 12:14-26)

The game, although reasonably simple, must be thought through carefully by the leader before trying it out. One youth group used three different "bodies" and three different keys on the trunk, representing "Faith, Hope and Love." The possibilities are great with a little creativity.

THE TRAVELING SALESMAN'S WIFE

For a great discussion starter on the subject of values and situation ethics, tell the following story (ad lib, don't read) and use a blackboard to diagram the people and places involved.

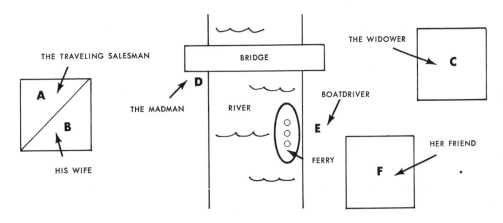

The Story:

Once upon a time there lived a couple (A and B) who had been married several years. A, the husband, was a traveling salesman who had to be away from home a great deal, often as much as 12 to 15 hours a day. B was the salesman's wife, who was forced to spend many lonely hours at home. One night A and B found time to attend a cocktail party at which another man, C, a widower who lived across the river, became friendly with A's wife, B, and began seeing her regularly. B was flattered as well as gradually finding herself falling in love with C. She would journey across the river (via the bridge) several times a week to visit C at his house where they would secretly make love. Because her husband (A) was very jealous, B was very careful to return home by 6:00 when A would come home for dinner, or phone from wherever he was. Thus, A never knew that B was seeing C, and the marriage was preserved.

One day, while B was across the river at C's house, a madman, D, climbed the bridge and began shooting at people crossing the bridge. The police blocked the bridge and would let no one cross. When B tried to return home, she found she could not cross the bridge due to the mad sniper. She went instead to the ferryboat which was the only other way across the river. When she tried to board the ferry, she found she had no money and could not pay the $1.50 toll. The ferryboat driver, E, refused her passage, despite much begging and pleading on the part of B. Time was running short, so B thought of a friend F, who lived near the ferryboat dock, who might possibly loan the money needed to cross the river. F, however, refused to loan B the money because she was aware of B's immoral conduct with C and felt it would be also immoral for her to loan the money, helping B to continue her relationship with C. Now B was getting panicky, knowing A would soon be returning home and discover she was gone, so she decided to take her chances on the bridge. She drove through the police barricade and sped across the bridge despite warnings and orders to halt. The madman, D, carefully took aim and shot B as she tried to cross, and B's car plunged into the river below, killing her instantly.

After Telling the Story, Ask:

1. Who was most responsible for B's death? List them in order.

    A. The husband, who made her lonely.
    B. The woman herself.
    C. The widower, who made love to her.
    D. The madman, who shot her.
    E. The ferryman, who wouldn't let her cross.
    F. The friend, who wouldn't loan the money.
    G. Anyone else (such as the police; or society — who created the madman).

Discuss the students' rating, asking why the judgments were made.

2. Rate the characters in the story from "best" to "worst." Again discuss the choices made, and allow students to defend their choices.

3. How could the woman's death have been prevented? List the best ways.

4. Which character do you most identify with? Have you ever found yourself in a similar situation? Would you have acted differently?

5. In what ways can "little sins" lead to big trouble? Give examples of this from your own experience. Is it ever safe to "bend" your convictions?

6. On what basis can we make "correct" decisions? Are there always "answers" available that we can use in lieu of having to make our own choices? Can we ever make choices without considering the "mitigating circumstances" or possible long range effects of those choices? Does the "end" ever justify the means?

PRAYER SURVEY

The following survey should be printed up and passed out to the entire group. Each person simply marks an "X" on each line to show his relative position on the issues presented. Encourage kids to be as honest as possible. There are no correct answers in this test. The idea is to see just where you stand on the various questions that come up regarding prayer.

POSITIVE	1	2	3	4	5	6	7	8	9	10	NEGATIVE
I believe beyond a shadow of a doubt that God answers prayer.											I believe there is a God but I question whether He is personally interested in man.
I don't always know how God answers prayers but I always have faith He will.											If I don't see an obvious answer I begin to wonder if God answers at all.
I often praise and thank God as well as petition Him.											I treat God like a Santa Claus. Give me this, give me that.
When God says, "No," I feel it is for my own good.											I can hardly accept a no answer.
When God answers a prayer my faith is strengthened.											"Answered prayer" in a book is just a coincidence.
If God says, "Wait awhile," I accept His timing without reservation.											I prayed once and God never answered, so I don't pray anymore.
I find myself praying all during the day.											Days go by and I never pray.
When I don't feel like praying that's when I pray the hardest.											If I don't feel like praying then I don't.
I feel as comfortable praying in public as I do alone.											I won't pray in public.
I feel my prayer life is really growing.											I've almost buried my prayer life.

The survey can be followed up by having all those consistently on the "positive" side of the continuum get together in one group and the "negatives" get into another group. Then have the two groups discuss the statements on page 96 as to their validity.

One group tries to convince the other, offering examples, personal experience, scripture and other proof.

1. God does answer prayer.
2. God answers prayer in one of three ways. Yes, no, or wait.
3. There are conditions to a yes answer.
4. A mature Christian needs to pray without ceasing.
5. Prayer shouldn't be governed by feelings.
6. The importance of public prayer.

CONTRIBUTORS

Allchin, Ron
Atom, Prince
Babington, Dick
Barwick, Tom
Berkley, Jim
Bransby, Dave
Brinkly, Torrey
Broadhurst, Sue
Cane, Brett
Copeland, Roger
Cox, Paul
Dietz, Gene
Elder, Dallas
Elliot, Ron
Enns, Paul
Erekson, Homer
Geckeler, Keith
Gilliam, Dave
Gleason, Bob
Graham, Neil
Grey, Tom
Griffis, Jay
Grindle, Jim
Harrower, Ken
Head, Nancy Lee

Heirendt, Dwight
Hockaday, Robert C.
Houseman, Larry
Janse, Larry
Kinloch, Greg
Liddle, Gary
Mees, Arthur
Mehaffie, Sam
Miglioratti, Phil
Moore, Wm.
Morgan, Steve
Nicodemus, Ron
O'Connor, Bill
Otto, Bruce
Paige, Roger
Parke, Dave
Pearce, Jr., Bryan
Powell, John
Ray, J. D.
Redwind, Alyce
Reynolds, Richard
Riggle, Steve
Robbings, Alvie
Schitt, W. Clarence

Shows, Scotty
Simmon, John
Smithtro, Shirley
Snider, Don
Splinter, John
Stevenson, Pete
Stier, Bob
Stockin, Marcie
Thompson, Nancy
Torrey, Peter
Tozer, Rose
Treat, Dave
Trotter, Lewis E.
Unrath, Daniel
Voskuil, Roger
Walker, Marve
Walsleben, Marjorie
Warner, Glen
Washburn, John
Weaver, Mike
Wells, Ron
Winnerholm, Carol
White, Whitey
Wright, Joe